COMBAT READY

READY

How to Fight the Culture War

by
Lynn Stanley

Huntington House Publishers

Huntington House Publishers
P.O. Box 53788
Lafayette, Louisiana 70505

Library of Congress Card Catalog Number 94-77741
ISBN 1-56384-074-X

Dedication

This book was written out of love and concern for all children and is dedicated to the sweet innocence and purity of childhood and the preservation of the traditional family, as God ordained it to be.

Contents

Scripture

The godly have been swept from the land; not one upright man remains. All men lie in wait to shed blood; each hunts his brother with a net. Both hands are skilled in doing evil; the ruler demands gifts, the judge accepts bribes, the powerful dictate what they desire—they all conspire together. The best of them is like a brier, the most upright worse than a thorn hedge. The day of your watchmen has come, the day God visits you. Now is the time of their confusion. . . . But as for me, I watch in hope for the Lord, I wait for God my Savior; my God will hear me.

—Micah 7:2–4, 7

1

Facing the Enemy

A sound of battle is in the land, and of great destruction.
—Jeremiah 50:22

The doors of the Hamilton Square Baptist Church rattled violently under the fists of the rioters. With faces contorted by rage, militant homosexuals shouted over the pounding sounds of their own fists against the hardwood doors. "Give us your children!" they screamed. "We want your children!"

A young mother looked around nervously, tightening the grip on her nine-year-old's hand. The small boy jerked his head up at her, his eyes filled with panic: "They're after me, Mama! It's *me* they want!" As worshippers inside the church stood frozen with fear, homosexual rioters hurled verbal obscenities through the windows. Even the strongest in the congregation flinched at the sounds of cement benches crashing into the fountain outside. Through the windows the congregation watched helplessly as rioters ripped street numbers from the church wall, trampled the landscape, and tore the Christian flag from its pole, replacing it with one of their own.

It was 19 September 1993. Pastor David Innes had invited a special guest speaker to the hundred-year-old church in San Francisco. The speaker was the Reverend Lou Sheldon of the Traditional Values Coalition, and he was scheduled to speak about the growing threat of the homosexual agenda. For obvious reasons, Rev. Sheldon's appearance had not been announced publicly in the bay area. Nevertheless, the news of his visit had somehow been broadcast throughout the homosexual community. A few threats had been leveled at the church leadership during the week preceding Sheldon's arrival, but such a violent incursion of activists had not been imagined. When Pastor Innes arrived at the church at 5:00 P.M. to prepare for the 6:00 P.M. service, he was met by a mob of angry homosexuals who challenged Rev. Sheldon's right to free speech and violated the human rights of every person present at Hamilton Square Baptist Church.

The sizable and violently aggressive crowd of homosexuals had come to demand that Rev. Sheldon not be allowed to speak. When he saw the mob outside the church, Rev. Innes immediately phoned the Northern Police Station and requested protection for his congregation. Even as he spoke on the phone, the number of protesters outside the church was growing at an alarming rate.

The police dispatcher was unimpressed by the reverend's urgent plea for help. "You must understand," she condescended, "that this is *San Francisco!*"

So for nearly two hours, Rev. Innes and his entire congregation were held hostage inside the walls of the church, as homosexuals vented their anger and frustration outside. When their rage finally exhausted them, they left, warning all within earshot that they'd be back. When the congregation calmed itself enough to go outside and survey the damage, they felt like soldiers canvassing a battlefield after combat. Literally, the church grounds had been ravaged.

The homosexuals had committed a myriad of crimes:

trespassing on private property, vandalism, and disturbing the peace, just to name a few—all of their crimes had been captured on videotape. Yet later, when Rev. Innes sought restitution for the damages to his church, he would learn that even though he had the videotape and even though members of the San Francisco Police Department had witnessed the riot, not a single arrest had been made.

Like the congregation at the Hamilton Square Baptist Church, the traditional American family is under siege—held captive by the many forces of evil that are allowed to march, unchecked, through the streets of our cities. Clearly, the house of cards known as "ethical pluralism" is collapsing, as we realize with painful clarity that neutrality in any sphere is a myth.

Ethical pluralism (or secular humanism) is the belief that there are no moral absolutes, that every act and circumstance depends upon the view of the individuals involved. Every aspect of ethical pluralism is contrary to biblical teaching and, yes, contrary to the viewpoint of our Founding Fathers who wrote the Constitution of the United States of America. Quite clearly, ethical pluralism is destroying the fiber of our culture and the survival of this great nation. Those who seek a return to the moral and ethical values upon which this country was established must get off the fence and take a bold stand for righteousness. We must contend for our Constitution and the rights granted us therein, in the same way we are forced to contend for our faith.

Painfully, many churches have shunned civic involvement in the past, thinking it contrary to the purpose of spreading the gospel. Now, those same churches are beginning to realize that the government they once trusted has been co-opted by the enemies of God. Suddenly, Christians realize that government is not the neutral agency they imagined it to be, given the doctrine of our Constitution. From the very beginning, government in America was consciously Judeo-Christian. America is a nation founded upon biblical principles, with the Ten Commandments predicating its moral law. Today, government has become consciously humanistic, and the political pursuit of ethical pluralism has gotten the better of common sense.

On videotape, tens of millions of people watched two young men from South Central Los Angeles crush a man's skull with a brick, yet a jury found them not guilty. When interviewed after the verdict, jurors expressed the opinion that the two were not guilty because they were black, poor, and oppressed. Therefore, in the eyes of the jury, they could not be held accountable for their actions.

The entire world was struck by the story of a woman who flew into a rage, grabbed a kitchen knife, and severed her husband's penis. She claimed temporary insanity, due to abuse at the hands of her husband. A few weeks earlier, the husband had been tried and found not guilty of sexual assault and battery. Still, the defendant walked away a free woman.

In Los Angeles, two brothers boldly confessed to murdering their parents in cold blood, then going on a spending spree with their multimillion-dollar inheritance. However, at this writing, neither jury in the separate trials was morally able to hand down a conviction. Both trials, which have already cost taxpayers more than two million dollars, ended in hung juries because jurors failed to agree that murdering one's parents is a punishable offense.

Thanks to the diabolical agenda of the National Education Association and its philosophically humanistic founders, we are dealing with generations of people who have been taught since kindergarten that there are no moral absolutes, and, if the circumstances merit, any behavior is acceptable. From school board meetings to legislative hearing rooms, from courtrooms to living rooms lit only by a flickering blue tube, the battle between the Christian world view and secular humanism has escalated into a full-scale war, leaving us to ask ourselves: How did it get this far? How did our nation become so violent, so full of hate, so misdirected? How did it happen, that what used to be considered "wrong" is now "right"?

There are two camps at war in this battle for the heart and soul of America. In the one camp are those who believe in moral absolutes; in the other are those who do not. (To those who think rationally the argument is moot because humanists say there are "absolutely" no absolutes!) As battle lines are drawn, those who win the cultural war will win the mind and conscience of this nation and, thus, chart its course toward greatness—or destruction.

Those arming themselves in the camp of moral absolutes are those who believe in God's judgment of man and His promise of an eternal life, either in heaven or in hell. For those who reverence God, the consequences we face for the fallen state of our nation are obvious. By contrast, forces in the camp of secular humanism (ethical pluralism) do not believe in the God of the Bible, nor do they fear His judgment. The only boundaries for humanists are those which individuals draw for themselves. Adolf Hitler drew wider boundaries than did the vast majority of secular humanists, but the underlying philosophy is the same: When man makes his own rules, anything is acceptable because right and wrong only exist as each individual defines them. Because Hitler truly believed that his philosophy regarding a perfect race was "good" and "right," pure humanist thought would find nothing wrong with the Holocaust because humanists believe that all morality is relative—nothing is absolutely "right," or absolutely "wrong." If asked, most humanists would reject that statement, but the fact remains that one can't have it both ways; there are either moral absolutes, or there aren't. If there are moral absolutes in one circumstance, there must be moral absolutes in all.

Likewise, humanist philosophy dictates that one should not be punished for breaking ethical or moral laws he perceives to be unfair. Humanists are teaching our children that, sometimes, theft is excusable; sometimes, murder is acceptable; lying is all right, if the situation merits. Again, from a humanist's perspective, whether or not a thing is acceptable is entirely up to the one breaking the moral law. By contrast, those who recognize biblical morality know that stealing is never excusable, murder is never acceptable, and lying is always wrong. That's not to say that Christians wouldn't do those things (as in times of war); it's only to admit that Christians agree that such behaviors are a violation of God's moral code and that God will ultimately judge them for their disobedience.

The religion of secular humanism is being forced upon our children through the public school system, even though our Constitution forbids that. Consequently, we have a nation of children growing up without boundaries, running wild through what once were the fences of morality and into the streets where they are murdering each other over clothing and boyfriends and school competitions. The same children who were taught in kindergarten that it's all right to steal food if you're hungry are now stealing car stereos because they're bored. Kids who have been taught that anything is acceptable "as long as it doesn't hurt anyone else" are sadly learning that all sin hurts someone. Every child who engages in random sex with multiple partners will probably suffer a broken heart, shattered self-esteem, or a sexually transmitted disease— and those are the "lucky" ones. The unlucky are contracting HIV, having babies they can't care for, or destroying human life through abortions. For every child who steals, someone experiences loss. For every child who murders, a life is lost, and the families of both the victim and the criminal are changed forever. For every lie that is told, someone suffers or becomes angry when the deception is revealed.

Failure to acknowledge the moral absolutes set forth in God's Word frees the humanist from the fear of consequences. "If there is no hell," he reasons, "if the afterlife is just a myth, why not live for the moment?" Where moral absolutes exist, morality is dictated by a holy God. In a world where moral absolutes do not exist, there is no gauge by which to measure morality and no Righteous Judge to hold man accountable for his actions. Instead, morality is dictated by man, and therein lies the problem we face today. When the boundaries of acceptability are constantly being stretched by individuals with varying value systems, the result is a nation of confused individuals. Where ethical pluralism exists, morality can be dictated by people as diverse in their beliefs as Abraham Lincoln and Adolf Hitler. In an ethically pluralistic society, right and wrong are constantly being redefined because the individuals giving the definitions always change. Again, Adolf Hitler is a perfect example. What he did was completely, absolutely wrong when viewed from a biblical perspective; but, within the context of the society he created, his actions were acceptable to an entire nation because he was within the boundaries of the moral code as *he* defined it to exist.

There will always be those who stand in opposition to God. God, Himself, gave us the right to oppose Him by virtue of the free will He granted to all men and women. Those who oppose biblical morality have a right to do so. But, they do not have the right to impose their values on the rest of society.

Why are proponents of homosexuality being allowed to force that perversion on those who oppose it? Why must public school students who believe in sexual abstinence be forced to attend classes that teach that sex outside of marriage (and with multiple partners) is normal and acceptable? Why must our children suffer the humiliation and embarrassment of sitting through co-ed classes in which discussions detail various sexual perversities and even instruct young men how to put on condoms? Why should children who believe in the concept of sin be force-fed the doctrine that, "according to individual circumstances, anything can be acceptable"? If this is truly a free country, how did it happen that Christian children lost their right to pray in the same public schools that openly encourage the practice of Eastern meditation?

Society cannot have order unless there is one consistent set of rules for every person and unless all people are judged equally according to those rules. The Word of God was set down for man, and the Word of God never changes. Since biblical times, the Bible has formed the foundation of societal law, with the Ten Commandments disposing the basis of morality throughout Western civilization. Indeed, the United States of America was founded by men who believed enough in the God of the Bible to fight for their religious freedom.

In this country established on biblical principles, Christians are being denied the right to speak in public forums and, thus, to exercise their Constitutional rights. The mention of Jesus Christ is forbidden in most public school forums, but discussion of alternative religious philosophies is always welcomed. While the distribution of Bible tracts is often prohibited near public schools, homosexual activists freely distribute pornographic brochures that graphically illustrate the proper way to put on a condom. Indeed, many of the sex education textbooks used in public schools today are as explicit as commercial pornography. Homosexuals have full access to campuses and use that time to indoctrinate our children into their "alternate lifestyle," while clergy and lay people who believe in traditional biblical morality are forbidden equal time.

Newly aware of these imminent moral dangers to their children, and fearing the extinction of traditional families and biblical morality, parents are looking desperately to the Church for direction and moral leadership and, too often, they find none. There's an illusion in the Church today that the collapse of society won't affect our children if we just keep them safely shielded behind the four walls of the church. Consequently, church youth leaders remain distracted in their efforts to find innovative ways to entertain our teens when they should, instead, be concentrating on teaching the Word of God. While the church is entertaining teens with music, games, and basketball leagues, the forces of evil are conspiring to destroy them by feeding our kids a doctrine of "safe sex" when medical research shows us clearly that *there is no such thing*. Our government is legally placing condoms into the hands of children with no thought given to the consequences: If your child becomes pregnant or contracts AIDS after using a government-distributed condom which fails, that same government will leave your son or daughter alone to deal with the consequences.

There are many battles to fight, and, on every front, our children are the spoils of war: the homosexual political movement can only survive if it preys on a new generation. Planned Parenthood is dependent upon the decay of our youth to maintain its billion-dollar abortion and condom industry. The National Education Association is making guinea pigs out of our children as it rewards mediocrity and manipulates the minds and value systems of our youth through its promotion of the Outcome-Based Education curriculum. As Hollywood and Madison Avenue continue to fill the minds of our children with violence and gratuitous sex, we have, in Janet Reno, an attorney general who actually conspires to push legislation through Congress that is sympathetic toward child pornographers. Every day, parents find their backs to the wall as they are forced to duel with the likes of Phil Donahue, Sally Jessy Raphael, and even cartoon characters like Bart Simpson and Beavis and Butthead, for the souls of their children. And sadly, in many cases, parents are losing out to the ethical pluralism that has even invaded the evangelical church.

Recently, the professor of a leading Christian college showed up to give a lecture to a large body of students, proudly wearing a prochoice pin. Several Christian colleges have implemented hate-speech codes, which restrict any negative reference to the homosexual lifestyle; if the codes are enforced, students and teachers can be disciplined for even suggesting that homosexuality is wrong.

While "Christian" colleges are endorsing the formation of gay alumni associations, God's Word, which never changes, says homosexuality is "detestable" (Lev. 18:22) and that those who engage in homosexuality will never enter the Kingdom of God (1 Cor. 6:9). Throughout the country, leaders of colleges and churches professing to follow Christ do not have the fortitude to take a stand against this most grievous sin because to take such a stand would be "politically incorrect."[1]

Such Christian colleges are devoting entire sections of their libraries to authors who have submitted to the demands of militant homosexuals and feminists, authors known to deny the virgin birth and the blood Atonement, New Age authors who have gotten "in touch with the God inside themselves" and compromised Scripture in order to win acceptance and sell books in an amoral society. Once dedicated to the Word of God, these people have been lured from the Truth by the philosophies of men and now condone that which is clearly opposed in Scripture. Though they call themselves Christians, these men and women are dividing the Body of Christ and depleting our forces on the spiritual battleground. Of these men and women, Scripture says, "They must be silenced because they are ruining whole households by teaching things they ought not to teach—and that for the sake of dishonest gain" (Titus 1:11).

One cannot assume that because a book is purchased from a Christian bookstore or borrowed from a Christian library, that all doctrines therein are Christian. Everything that's written must be weighed against the inerrant truth contained in God's Word, the Bible. Certainly, this is a free country, and one can write whatever one pleases. Authors can bend and twist and contort the Word of God until it says just what society wants to hear. But, those who know the truth are aware of the fate awaiting anyone who attempts to alter or reinterpret the Word of God. What man says is opinion; what God says is fact—we must never confuse the two.

It's oppressive to deal with issues like sexual perversions and promiscuity because those things are evil and destructive to human lives. Further, it is oppressive to consider the injustice being done to our children in the name of public school education. This poses the question, "Why write a book like this?" After all, the Bible says we should think of that which is true, noble, right, pure, lovely, admirable, and praiseworthy (Phil. 4:8). It's important to note that the first designation is to that which is true. Though this text considers what is true, certainly none of the subjects covered are noble or right or any of those other adjectives. But, Scripture also warns us to be as "shrewd" as the enemy, and shrewdness implies that we need to be informed. Indeed, the Lord has appointed watchmen (Ezek. 33:6) to warn His people of approaching danger; the danger is no longer approaching—it is here.

Scripture tells us to be informed, but not to be unduly concerned with the affairs of this world. With that in mind, we should not dwell on sin until it becomes so oppressive that it ruins our lives, but neither should we just ignore it. One could equate the denial of the moral collapse of this nation to knowing that a murderer is stalking your family: Ignoring the danger won't change the fact that someone is out to destroy you. In order to protect yourself, you must be able to identify the enemy. You must know where the enemy is, and you must know as much about him as possible, so you can build an adequate defense against him.

Certainly, if we considered only the negative implications of society today, we would be overwhelmed by the task stretched out before us. Much of what you will read in the following pages will shock you. Some of it will even horrify you and make you red with rage. Some of the information contained in these pages will make you cry from frustration, and some of it will cause you great anxiety if you do not remember that "greater is He who is in you, than He who is in the world" (John 4:4).

Those who trust in God and believe His promises will find it possible to consider the sin that exists in the world—and even to examine it closely—and still be joyful in the Lord. For those who know the Word of God and obey it, there is no reason to fear, no cause for anxiety, and no reason to lose hope. On the contrary, our hope is in Him to deliver our children—and our nation—out of the hands of the enemy. This book was not written out of frustration and panic, but out of the knowledge that with Christ, all things are possible, and those who contend for the faith will be blessed and will stand strong until the end. As Christians in these difficult times, we must be united, and we must be informed. Most of all, we must be focused on Jesus Christ and reliant on the power and promises of our God, who says, "Blessed is the man who perseveres under trial, because when he has stood the test, he will receive the crown of life" (James 1:12).

Endnotes

1. Andrés Tapia, "Homosexuality Debate Strains Campus Harmony," *Christianity Today* (22 November 1993): 38-40.

2

The National Education Association

Cursed is the one who trusts in man, who depends on flesh for his strength and whose heart turns away from the Lord. . . . But blessed is the man who trusts in the Lord, whose confidence is in him.

—Jeremiah 17:5, 7

Schools will become clinics whose purpose is to provide individualized psycho-social treatment for the student, and teachers must become psycho-social therapists. Children are to become the objects of experimentation.

—*Education for the Seventies*, an NEA pamphlet

Precursor of Crisis

There is no question that this nation faces a public education crisis. Since 1965, Scholastic Aptitude Test scores have steadily declined. Though the United States spends more than $400 billion annually on education, a recent report issued by the U.S. Department of Education (September 1993) shows that "*47% of adult Americans demonstrate low levels of literacy.*" In February of 1992, *Education Week* reported that U.S. students ranked fifteenth in a twenty-nation study in the subject of science and even worse in math. It's almost impossible to imagine how the greatest nation on earth—the country most generously blessed with freedom, prosperity, and opportunity for everyone—has come to lag behind countries like Ireland, Jordan, and Portugal in academic achievement, with our national education standards among the lowest in the entire world.

Certainly, the failure of any system—whether it be education or the failure of society as a whole—cannot be attributed to one single cause. But always, there is one organization, one person, or one philosophy that works as an impetus for everything that follows. In the case of education, the National Education Association (NEA) is the harbinger of the crisis we face today; to understand where America went wrong, one must first understand the philosophy and tactic of the NEA. Through these pages, the reader will see how the NEA has slowly circumvented the American people until, suddenly, the disastrous results of its philosophies have come full circle, entrapping us all. From the NEA's birth in 1857, to the introduction of the U.N. Convention on the Rights of the Child in 1989, one can view the life of the NEA and the death of American society.

In doing research for this chapter, parents were asked to define the National Education Association and to explain what they believed the function of that organization to be. Almost without exception, those familiar with the NEA said they thought it was designed to make education better. Most thought the NEA was dedicated to establishing curriculum in our public schools that would enable their children to become better readers, more proficient mathematicians, and good citizens. Some parents believed the NEA is struggling to keep America's public schools competitive with those in the rest of the world, and others said they thought the NEA was simply a teacher's union—those respondents gave the most cause for concern because they are so obviously deceived regarding the truth about the NEA and its hidden agenda.

It's true that the NEA is a teacher's union; it grew out of the premise that there was a need to promote the professional interests of all teachers in America. In addition, the NEA claimed to provide a method for gathering statistics so the progress of students within the school system could be measured. By 1944, the NEA implemented a plan to unify *all* teachers, and those living in states that adopted the plan were (and still are) *forced* to join the NEA, whether or not they shared the liberal philosophies of the organization's founders. Today, the NEA is arguably the most powerful political lobby in the United States, with more than two million members—literally, with enough votes to control the political destiny of America. At this writing, twelve thousand NEA units are in place, controlling every school district in the country. It's imperative to understand that the National Education Association is much more than a teacher's union. From its inception, the purpose of the NEA has never been to create literate Americans; a study of the organization's history proves that the purpose has always been to re-educate America toward socialization. The NEA is a philosophically socialist organization, and, as such, it has been the driving force behind the socialist reforms we see in the United States today. A socialistic America and the ultimate acceptance of a socialist, global government ("The New World Order") is now, and always has been, the ultimate goal of the National Education Association.

Though all teachers certainly do not agree with the radical ideas and political philosophies of the educational elite who direct the NEA, many of them—even Christians—consider the organization's concept of Outcome-Based Education a boon to the public schools. Unfortunately, few have studied the issue in depth, sincerely questioned the value of the new curriculum, or thought carefully enough about its moral implications to equate the

obvious: The steady decline in academic test scores corre-
lates directly to the introduction of OBE curricula (formerly, "Behavior Modification" or "Mastery Learning")
and the accompanying teaching methods endorsed by the
NEA. Scholastic Aptitude Test scores declined steadily
from 1951 to 1980, plummeting by as much as ninety
points before they began to rise, slightly. The improvement in scores can be attributed to an NEA-inspired
phenomenon called "grade inflation," now referred to as
the "dumbing down" of America. School work formerly
worthy of a "C" grade was suddenly deserving of an "A,"
as the NEA made a futile attempt to prove that children
were still learning. In addition, the U.S. Department of
Education reported a 17 percent increase in private school
enrollment, as more and more parents began to realize
that public education wasn't getting the job done.

OBE concepts have been introduced so subtly, and
teachers of the future have been indoctrinated so insidiously, that most do not recognize the ultimate danger of
the radical changes taking place. Dr. Shirley McCune, a
major proponent of OBE, made its goal perfectly clear
when addressing the Governor's Conference on Education in 1989. There, she openly admitted that the NEA "is
into a total restructuring of the society." Sadly, it was at
that same conference that implementation of Goals 2000
became the aspiration of most of the governors in attendance.

Since the introduction of OBE, there has only been
one school district reporting an improvement in academic
test scores following use of the curriculum, and that district has three extremely unique advantages over most
others: The Johnson City, New York, school district pays
for two weeks of staff training each summer, and they pay
for tutors to help the slower children so the more advanced students don't have to wait for them to catch up.
In addition, classroom size averages one teacher for each
fifteen students. But, for that one exception, OBE has
been a miserable failure at improving literacy skills in

every school district where it has been used. In spite of that fact, the Clinton administration imposed mandatory Outcome-Based Education for every public school in America through the Goals 2000 legislation (explained in depth in the following chapter).

Now more than ever, parents want to know why public education has been allowed to run so far amuck. They want—and deserve—to know who's most responsible for the education crisis in America, and they want those people held accountable. Further, taxpayers want to know why they must continue to pour $493 billion dollars annually into a department of education that isn't effectively teaching their children simple math and reading skills.

The NEA's Legacy

By 1960, the NEA was an educational force to be reckoned with. Since they receive the bulk of the more than $400 billion dollars Uncle Sam spends on education each year, it's important to know what their significant contributions to education have been since then. According to Grapevine Publications Network of Boise, Idaho, here's how the NEA stacks up from 1960 to 1992:

Spending per student has increased, 535%.
SAT scores have declined, 76%.
Teenage pregnancies have doubled.
Teen suicides have tripled; attempted suicides are up 500%.
They boast 2.1 million members, and control every aspect of public education.
They approved the removal of prayer, the Bible, and the Ten Commandments from our schools.
Violent Crime is up 57%. (*USA Today*, 17 March 1994)

Further, the number of functional illiterates has almost doubled—up to 40 million from 23 million in 1960. Now, that's worth funding!

The History of the NEA

A brief analysis of the history of the NEA will demonstrate why the public education system is failing and why the NEA wants to force Outcome-Based Education upon our children, even though they know it does not adequately prepare them for the future.

The NEA was founded in 1857 by a group of socialist educators who firmly believed that schools should be owned and controlled by the government. These original founders preferred the old Prussian system of education—strongly committed to spiritual neutrality and statism—and demanded that parents surrender the rights of their children in favor of the (supposed) greater rights of the state. That explains why the NEA and OBE curricula have no place for God and little tolerance for parental involvement.

John Dewey was a founder of the NEA and the architect of much of its agenda. Dewey was the father of the Progressive Education movement and considered himself a "social educator." As a progressive, Dewey thought existing classrooms were rigid and detached from reality; he favored classrooms with less structure, where students and teachers had a more casual relationship. The goal of the progressives was to define "useful" subjects and then to create schools that taught those subjects. As Progressive Education evolved over the years, it became apparent that progressives did not consider subjects like reading and math as "useful" as subjects on human sexuality and moral relativism.

John Dewey was instrumental in introducing behaviorism and, subsequently, behavior modification (now known as Outcome-Based Education) into the public school system. He was a model socialist who loudly protested biblical orthodoxy and described his method of teaching as "learning by doing." He then deemed himself qualified to reinvent the entire public school system. He then ordained members of the NEA to adjust curriculum according to the need of the individual child—as the NEA defined that need. Most significantly, Dewey de-emphasized the importance of cognitive skills—skills needed to reason and develop rational thought—and began to concentrate on the development of the student's personality. Instead of teaching children to develop their thought processes, Dewey and his followers began to tell them what to think. "Teach the child," Dewey said, "not the subject." By altering public school curriculum, Dewey claimed authority for himself and his disciples to change the thoughts, feelings, and actions of America's children.

In 1896, Dewey became head of the departments of philosophy, psychology, and education at the University of Chicago. There, he was allowed a prestigious forum for his ideas when he created the Laboratory School and started his experiments on children. He began to teach reading, writing, and arithmetic as one would teach chemistry or biology—adjusting curricula, like formulas, in order to test philosophies and ideas on live children. In essence, Dewey used children like guinea pigs. It is important to note: the goal of Dewey's Laboratory School was not to teach basic literacy skills, but to prove that by manipulating children's minds, he could get them to behave in specific ways, even to the point of changing the way they viewed society. Through his Laboratory School, Dewey very subtly challenged educators to transform America into a socialist society—because that's what he thought was best for all of us. So, you see, Outcome-Based Education is nothing new; it's simply a snake that keeps growing new skin.

As the NEA became the dominant force in education, it ventured further into the field of behaviorism, continually changing curricula to accommodate a science limited to the study and quantification of only that which can be seen. Behaviorism is a humanistic science that does not allow for the supernatural and, thus, eliminates the God of the Bible and the concept of divine creation. Thus, the NEA discarded as *useless* the development of cognitive skills associated only with human intelligence, and replaced them with a method of training through social and motor skills—outcome-based methods commonly associated with the training of animals.

The Philosophy of the NEA

The NEA offers membership to most professional groups engaged in the business of education. As the number of special-interest groups within the NEA grew, the National Council of Education (NCE) was formed to oversee them all. Like the NEA, the NCE was founded by an elitist group of educators who were equally propelled by a resolute faith in science and a seeming contempt for the Bible. In their efforts to discredit Scripture, these early educators quickly embraced Dewey's philosophies, Darwin's theory of evolution, and the subsequent religion of humanism, which believes that the supernatural does not exist. The founders of the NEA and NCE had no use for the supernatural God of the Bible. They immediately sought to eliminate biblical teaching from public schools— a ludicrous act when one considers the original premise behind public education in the United States. Our Founding Fathers deemed literacy an imperative, so all citizens could read the Scriptures! Subtly, though, the NEA has succeeded in eliminating God and replacing the Truth with a doctrine of salvation through science and education—a trend that continues today and is of great concern to those who hold firmly to the biblical precepts upon which our nation was founded.

Traditional American values are constantly under attack by the NEA, which focuses largely on teaching "values education" as *they* determine values to be. In their publication, "Values and Valuing Parents and Students," the NEA admits that parents "may wonder if values education is valid if it leads young people to explore and analyze, rather than accept, the traditional values of our society." It is becoming more and more apparent that the NEA's idea of values consists largely of validating the same behaviors that have caused society problems throughout history. In its quest for a "values-neutral" society, the NEA has partnered with homosexual activists and Planned Parenthood to create and endorse "educational" materials that are anything *but* neutral. Essentially the equivalent of pornography, courses conceived in back alleys are being offered under the deceptive titles of "health" and "family," while traditional biblical morality is never mentioned as a choice to be considered.

From the beginning, the humanist founders of the NEA have fought vigorously to replace biblical Christianity with the religion of secular humanism which is currently being taught in every public school in America. Though the NEA insists that humanism is "a philosophy, not a religion," the true definition of humanism is found in John Dewey's own *Humanist Manifesto 1*: "Humanism is a philosophical, *religious* and moral point of view" (emphasis added).[1] Even though the Constitution expressly forbids the establishment of a national religion, and even though the Supreme Court of the United States of America recognized humanism as a religion,[2] our government continues to force that religion on its citizens through public school curriculum, which is funded with taxpayer's money. This can happen only because the public is unaware of the fact that humanism is the unofficial religion of the NEA, and *that* philosophy is undeniably reflected in all the curricula the NEA endorses.

A child's mind is like a fresh canvas, ready to be painted with the colors of life. As with any work of art, the outcome depends upon who's got the brush. The most effective way to create change in the cultural landscape is to color the minds of children. Humanists know that the children of today are the socialists of tomorrow; thus, curriculum designed to evaluate children *philosophically* is the only goal of OBE. Courses that once challenged students to use their abilities to reason have been replaced with courses that encourage students to rely on others to do their thinking for them. Clearly, how a child feels about society has become more important to educators than the child's ability to survive independently in that society. By way of example, consider this excerpt from a textbook written for future teachers:

> The humanist curriculum features activities which are exploratory, puzzling, playful, and spontaneous—all of which are vital for innovation and self-renewal. The best interests of Americans lie in providing students with a curriculum that is fixed on the future—on what is possible and potential, not on what is merely utilitarian . . . or which will make the learner a helpless captive to what is already known. . . .

> Widespread dissatisfaction with much of the present curriculum is evidenced by high dropout rates, vandalism, and discipline problems among the bored, the unhappy, and the angry. . . . The humanistic curriculum addresses this concern. . . . When we consider the tools needed for employment, highest priority must be given to attitudes and human relations. The diminishing quality of job applicants is due more to their poor attitudes than to their lack of job skills.[3]

More absurd than the concept itself is the fact that the quote was taken from a text used to educate aspiring teachers! The text admits that 1) the humanistic curriculum is experimental, 2) basic reading, math, and communications skills are considered "merely utilitarian," 3) the humanist curriculum "addresses the concerns" of high dropout rates and severe disciplinary problems—*the very problems it admits it creates!* And, 4) humanists consider attitudes more important than job skills.

The argument that favors humanist curriculum defeats itself by admitting its own failure. Further, I challenge the author to produce a single employer who would prefer an illiterate employee with "a good attitude" (and, "good," by whose standards?) to one who communicates well through speech and written word and shows competency in the areas of math and reading skills. Indeed, who would go to an accountant who can't add or subtract, but "has a great attitude"? Who would hire a "self-renewed" cashier who can't make proper change or a carpenter who "thinks right," but never learned to calculate measurements? Indeed, if the humanist curriculum is such a boon to education, why are so many students "bored, unhappy, and angry"—by the author's own admission? Could it possibly be that the boredom, unhappiness, and anger result when all those young adults with "right attitudes" realize they're unemployable because they don't have the literacy skills necessary to survive in the business world?

Self-actualization (finding oneself) is at the heart of all humanistic curricula. Therefore, courses must give students opportunities to act out and experiment with the idea of "who he or she is." Thus, class time, once spent learning cognitive skills, is now spent in the student's examination of his "response to his life experiences." The focus is no longer on intellectual growth; it's on psychological growth and self-esteem. Outcome-based curriculum stresses growth that cannot be objectively measured, because the outcome depends on the point of view of the one doing the testing. The emphasis is on process, rather than product. By contrast, traditional curriculum teaches students to read, reason, and solve problems; it has criteria for achievement that can be objectively measured by testing: Can your child add? Subtract? Spell? Can he express himself cohesively? In contrast to OBE curriculum, traditional academic curriculum always produces "right" and "wrong" answers: Two plus two is always four; and no matter how many times one divides one hundred by five, the correct answer will always be twenty.

The Evolution of the NEA

To understand the tremendous impact the NEA has had on our personal lives and on our society in general, one must consider the steps they've taken over the last 137 years in their efforts to gain control of the minds of our children. In the late 1800s, the introduction of psychology into Teacher's College brought with it the temptation for educators like John Dewey to substitute experimentation for practiced methods of teaching. In their zealousness to prove man's connection to animals through evolution, educators stopped teaching and began to *train* our children. They abandoned the use of practice and intellectual exercises in learning and began to experiment with the same "learn by conditioning" methods that science was using to train laboratory animals. Over time, the pomposity of science got the better of common sense; instead of viewing man as more intelligent than animals, science redefined man as simply the most intelligent of them. Hence, man was considered just another animal, and classrooms became equivalent to scientific laboratories where children were reduced to learning by the same reflex conditioning and stimuli-response techniques used to train rats in a maze.

The most devastating effect of the NEA has been its assault on the traditional alphabetic-phonics method of teaching reading. Without consulting anyone—least of all parents—the NEA replaced the phonetic method of teaching with the look-say method. Look-say is blamed for the fact that most of the children who graduate from public high schools cannot read past the fifth-grade level. Look-say defies common sense, and the reason for its failure can be simply explained: The look-say (or "whole language") method of teaching reading is incompatible with the English language because it uses graphic symbols not related to the spoken word. In English, we use an alphabetic writing system. The phonetic method of teaching considers the sounds letters make, the way the letters are combined, and how they are represented by the written symbols of our alphabet. By contrast, look-say replaces words with pictures that can be interpreted any way the reader wishes. For example, imagine holding up a picture of a bird with the word "robin" written next to it. Your child considers the picture; but instead of reading the word "robin," he says the word, "bird." The logical thing would be to correct him; but according to Dr. Kenneth Goodman, an author of look-say textbooks and (understandably) one of OBE's leading proponents, it wouldn't matter if your child misread the word because "he got the meaning." (I wonder what Dr. Goodman would say if his six-year-old picked up a bottle marked "Poison" thinking it said "Pop"?)

While most parents agree that basic reading skills are an imperative foundation for good education, Dr. Goodman negates that belief and refers to reading as a "psycholinguistic guessing game."[4] If it doesn't send you into a rage to think that your tax dollars are paying for books written by this guy—and that your child could be learning to read from one of them—it should!

As early as 1929, declining test scores proved that the look-say method was ineffective and *actually hindered reading skills*. And, the NEA knew, way back then, that the imposition of look-say actually induced dyslexia in children because of its extreme incompatibility with our alphabetic writing system.[5] But, instead of returning to the phonetic method which was proven successful, the NEA began an even more aggressive drive to replace all phonetic reading curricula with look-say textbooks, beginning with the "Dick and Jane" series in 1930. Slowly and stealthily, all phonetically structured reading books were eliminated from schools and libraries.

By 1935, when the adverse effects of the look-say method became public knowledge, the NEA and the author of the "Dick and Jane" series, Dr. William Scott Gray, were left to explain the alarming decline in reading skills. Conveniently, Gray discovered a "whole new syndrome of problems that were causing reading disability: mental deficiency or retardation, defective vision, auditory deficiencies, congenital word blindness, developmental alexia, congenital aphasia, (the ever-popular) dyslexia, congenital alexia, strephosymbolia, cerebral dominance," etc., etc., etc.[6] In other words, Dr. Gray and the NEA blamed reading failure on everything but the actual cause—failure in the method of teaching. At the same time, the NEA took full advantage of the reading crisis they had created. Once they had parents distracted with worry over low reading scores and the myriad of "syndromes" miraculously discovered by Dr. Gray, the NEA justified the need for new reading texts so they could furtively change the content of the readers our children were using.

By the early 1950s, the NEA had rewritten textbooks (and sometimes history) and changed curricula to accommodate the "science" of behaviorism, where only the visible is considered. Taking full advantage of its authority to create curricula, the NEA insidiously saturated textbooks with socialist philosophies and humanist doctrine, paving the way for the godless, amoral curricula we see in some schools today. By way of example, compare this text from an early primary reader, circa 1920-1950, to the excerpts from current readers which follow:

1. Remember, child, remember, that God is in the sky; That He looks down on all we do, With an ever-wakeful eye.

2. Remember, oh remember, That, all the day and night, He sees our thoughts and actions With an ever-watchful sight.

3. Remember, child, remember, That God is good and true; That He wishes us to always be Like Him in all we do.

4. Remember that He ever hates A falsehood or a lie; Remember He will punish, too, The wicked, by and by.

5. Remember, oh remember, That He is like a friend, And wishes us to holy be, And happy, in the end.

6. Remember, child, remember, To pray to Him in heaven; And if you have been doing wrong, Oh, ask to be forgiven.[7]

Today, fourth-graders are learning to read, using text like this:

In flowing dress the sorceress begins her evil toil. She stirs her vat of filth and fat and sees it seethe and boil.

Midst hellish smells she whispers spells and does a deadly dance, with words of death upon her breath she slips into a trance.

Higher, higher burns her fire, distant is her voice, and Hades' hold takes one more soul as demons there rejoice.

In flowing dress the sorceress falls swooning to the floor—her brew grows cold, her tale is told, her victim lives no more.[8]

A second-grade reader tells the story of a "good" girl who "happily" mutilates herself: "She had lost the gift of the good star. What should she do? She wished to save her brothers and had no key to the glass mountain. The good little sister took a knife and cut off one of her fingers, stuck it in the door, and happily opened it."[9]

Reading primers today are void of educational content and littered with violence, occult themes, and encouragements to defy authority: "School was a sort of punishment. Parents always want to punish their children and school is their most natural way of punishing us."[10]

Science vs. Reality

No public school course is exempt from the secular humanist philosophy. While science says the only reality is that which can be observed, the Bible tells us that faith is being certain of what we do not see.[11] Because public education is based on the premise that there is no God, it relies on the theory of evolution to account for the origin of life and, thus, avoids any mention of divine creationism.

In his in-depth study of the NEA, Samuel L. Blumenfeld chronicled the history of the self-anointed saints of the humanist religion who appointed themselves heads over public education (members of the NCE). Referring to these early educators as "The Education Mafia," Blumenfeld says, "These were just a few of the men who created a network of control and influence that was to change the face of public education in America." According to Blumenfeld, in a period of less than ten years, the Education Mafia took control of the public schools from elected officials and placed it in the hands of professional educators, handpicked by the NEA. Largely through intimidation, that small but powerful group soon had local school superintendents understanding that the NEA was in charge of curriculum and that if they valued their jobs, they'd better conform. Soon, the whole nation was unwittingly conforming. For years, the NEA quietly and insidiously went about the business of infecting the public schools with their humanist philosophies, and no one even noticed.[12]

As early as 1928, membership in the NEA was significant enough to merit an effective lobby in Washington, which persuaded government to pour unprecedented amounts of money into public education. By the late 1950s, the governing board of the NEA made an overt appeal to its members to become actively involved in the political process in an effort to promote the organization's political agenda. Subsequently, power of the NEA was clearly felt in 1965, when the Johnson administration passed the Elementary and Secondary Education Act (ESEA), the largest aid-to-education package ever allocated by Congress. Once the NEA convinced Congress to pass the ESEA, tax dollars began flowing so rapidly into public education, that the government has never been able to control it. (Apparently, it costs a great deal more to "adjust children's attitudes," than it does to teach them to read and write.) For almost thirty years, unprecedented amounts of tax dollars have made it easy for the NEA to continue funding the experimental curricula they use on our children. The point should be made, that schools *never* cut back for lack of funds. Funding is more than adequate to educate every child in America. Schools are often forced to make cutbacks because the money they have is poorly managed or wasted on unnecessary "politically correct" programs with absolutely no academic value.

Following passage of the ESEA, Student Aptitude Test (SAT) scores dropped an astounding forty-eight points.[13] The decline has steadily continued, in spite of the 50 percent increase in spending in the last ten years, as reported in the *U.S. Department of Education News*, 3 September 1993. The reason for the decline, despite the dollars spent? Our children can't read! In 1983, the National Commission on Excellence in Education published a report titled, *A Nation at Risk: The Imperative for Educational Reform.* Through that report, the commission made known the desires of the majority, regarding public education: Parents want an end to behavioral experimentation in the classroom and a return to educational basics. They want more class time spent teaching English, math, science, social studies, and computer science, and they want tougher requirements in those subjects. In addition to more homework, parents want to see longer school days and a lengthened school year. They want stricter discipline in the classroom and tougher standards for teachers. In addition, parents want more challenging curricula and better textbooks. Following the release of that report and all the furor it created, parents erroneously

assumed that the NEA would listen, take corrective measures, and adjust curriculum accordingly. What we got,
instead, was more Outcome-Based Education—the same
curricula that are driving public education over the edge!

Through OBE, the NEA has determined to reengineer
society by radically changing what is taught in public
schools and how it's taught. As proof of that, consider
the following quote from a college textbook used to educate the teachers of the future: "A new left has evolved
that seeks social reforms *using the schools* to awaken allies
in labor, civil rights, and other groups with the need for
control and power" (emphasis added).[14] The "new left" is
not really new at all. It has, in fact, been at work within
the public schools since the NEA was created.

The obvious question is: Why would the NEA want
our children to be illiterate? The answer is simple: The
crisis in education today is the result of the NEA's desire
to create a socialistic America. Those who read gain knowledge. The literate man thinks, reasons, and questions
science and government. A literate person with cognitive
skills can study the facts and determine for himself whether
or not the theory of evolution is scientifically possible.
Even atheists agree that the only other alternative is divine creation. That understanding often brings skeptics
to the conclusion that God *does* exist, raising questions
about everything the NEA preaches regarding the absence of moral absolutes. An intelligent being will question philosophies; those who venture to think impede the
spread of the socialist agenda and the perpetuation of the
humanist dogma. Thus, the NEA has a keen interest in
keeping students illiterate. The socialist agenda dictates
that the masses be kept illiterate and subject to government for survival; thus, the increasing number of social
programs currently being hawked under the Clinton administration is elucidated. It's beyond belief to think that
the NEA has wasted hundreds of billions of our tax dollars to create a nation of illiterates—but that's exactly what
they've done.

How Did It Get This Far?

In their zealousness to force socialism on the citizens of the United States, the NEA furtively worked to change the minds of teachers. Eventually, the NEA rid itself of all who rebelled against its liberal philosophies. In the beginning, they dealt cautiously with educators who resisted radical change, most of which had to do with the NEA's method of teaching reading. (It should not be surprising that the subject of reading has been such a bone of contention between liberal and conservative educators; *knowledge is gained from reading*.) As the NEA continued its assault in the halls of education, many teachers became casualties. Some were quietly fired, others quit out of frustration, and some simply continued (under protest from the NEA) to teach the "old way" (phonetics) until they retired. And, as all of this was going on in local school districts throughout the country, the National Council of Education was firmly positioning its members in the finest institutions of higher learning in America, where they began to indoctrinate student teachers in the socialist-humanist philosophies of the NEA. As a result of that indoctrination, some of the most active and powerful advocates of the radical Left can now be found teaching in the public schools and state universities of this nation.

By the mid-1950s, our entire public school system was infected by the treacherous left-wing philosophies of the NEA, and a country founded upon biblical principles surreptitiously fell into the hands of a godless few. Equally alarming is the fact that they took over so slowly, so cunningly, and so thoroughly that most of us never saw it coming.[15] Without our knowledge, the NEA used the public school system to snatch our children right out of our grasp. They used our tax dollars to indoctrinate our children into a philosophical way of thinking that leaves no room for moral absolutes, refuses to acknowledge the existence of God, and has left more than 40 percent of our nation's children functionally illiterate.

As Samuel Blumenfeld reported, we can measure the success of the conspiracy against literacy in the United States by comparing two statistics: First, a U.S. Bureau of Education report published in 1915 which stated that in 1910 only one child out of every thousand between the ages of ten and fourteen in Massachusetts was illiterate. By contrast, in 1984, a *Boston Globe* editorial stated that "about 40% of the city's adult population is believed to be functionally illiterate."[16] Further, Blumenfeld quotes Professor Steven Marcus of Columbia University as writing that the problem of functional illiteracy is so out of control, it has become the job of higher education to use the first two years to repair the damage done in the primary and secondary grades.[17]

Cashing in on Disabilities

The terms "reading disabled" and "learning disabled" were not coined in the medical arena. The NEA assigned those labels to children it failed to educate so it could rid itself of the responsibility of performing the very function for which it was allegedly established—that being to improve the quality of public education. In 1975, a federal law was passed that guaranteed handicapped children the right to an education. So, the NEA determined to label as many students as possible "disabled" in order to receive additional tax dollars to "educate" those children. Literally, the NEA received hundreds of millions of *additional* tax dollars by labeling students "disabled" or "at risk." Since the 1975 law was passed, the number of "disabled" and "at risk" students has grown by more than 200 percent.

The NEA used some of its additional tax revenue to establish "special-ed" classes—a move that created hundreds of thousands of jobs for NEA members, in spite of the fact that public school enrollment had dropped by 12 percent. (Of the 1.7 million students receiving special-ed services during that time, 40 percent were deemed "learning disabled.")[18] Not surprisingly, the greatest increase in "learning disabilities" and "at risk" children has come from urban minority populations. There, the numbers of LD children have increased by as much as 496 percent since 1975. All told, special-ed classes cost taxpayers more than ten billion dollars a year, providing a financial benefit to the NEA which should concern us all.[19]

Significantly, the NEA has secured billions of tax dollars to fund programs that continue to fail. In effect, government is *paying* the NEA for not doing its job. Further, the terms "learning disabled" and "at risk" have been so broadly applied that, for all intents and purposes, the definition of an "at risk" child is left wide open and could include virtually any child. (For more information on "at risk" designations, see chapter 3 on Goals 2000.)

Change Agents

As the NEA story unfolds, it begins to read like a spy novel as tactics like the use of "Change Agents" are revealed. A Change Agent is any mechanism whereby government can transmit its ideology. The NEA is certainly a Change Agent, as are its many spinoff organizations, like the National Training Laboratory (NTL). The NTL was established for the sole purpose of "changing teachers' inflexible patterns of thinking." The organization manual says, "Although [children] appear to behave appropriately . . . they may actually be in need of mental health care in order to help them change, adapt, and conform to the planned society." The "society" the NTL is "planning" for is called "Socialism."[20] Organizations like the NTL then send their "retrained-teacher-graduates" into the classroom where they become Change Agents to our children. Thus, the radical socialist doctrine is introduced into the schools.

Parents are fed up with academic decline, curricula that psychologically manipulates their children, surveys and "tests" that invade the privacy of the family, and textbooks that are morally offensive. Parents are shouting loudly for reform, but, clearly, their shouts fall on the deaf ears of the NEA. Overwhelmingly, taxpayers have expressed their desire for a return to the basic academics. In short, parents want things the way they used to be, before SAT tests began an uninterrupted decline. What's really disturbing is that the very programs which parents view as failures are seen as successes by the NEA, whose very purpose is to keep our children illiterate. For example, look at what Harvard professor Anthony Oettinger has to say about the importance of literacy:

> The present "traditional" concept of literacy has to do with the ability to read and write. But the real question is: How do we help citizens function in society? . . . Do we really want to teach people to do a lot of sums or write in a fine round hand when they have a . . . calculator or a word processor to work with? . . . Do we really have to have everybody literate—writing and reading in the traditional sense?[21]

(Apparently, it's not as difficult to get into Harvard as everyone thought!)

If Professor Oettinger's statements don't scare you enough, the National Institute of Education's Thomas Sticht had this to say in the *Washington Post*: "Many companies have moved operations to places with cheap, relatively poorly educated labor. . . . Ending discrimination and changing values are probably more important than reading in moving low-income families into the middle class." No wonder the welfare roles keep growing! What most Americans view as the grave failure of education is considered a success to the socialist behaviorists who have seized control of public education.

How Curriculum Is Planned

Goals, objectives, textbooks, and other learning materials are federally financed and developed through universities and educational regional laboratories. In this arena, specialized personnel decide what will be taught and what teaching methods will be used. Individual states are then responsible for producing their own curriculum guides and frameworks within the context of what they receive from the federal government. (However, as you'll find in the next chapter, this may soon change, with the federal government assuming the right to control *all* curricula.) Usually, states appoint advisory committees composed of professional educators, representatives from educational agencies, and selected lay persons to formulate the curriculum.

Most curriculum decisions are made in individual school districts, where specialized personnel, teachers, consultants, and lay people decide what the children in their district will be taught. School boards usually adopt curricula that meet their individual needs and consider the implications of the region in which the school is located. Thus, the importance of electing school board members and selecting teachers who share your philosophical beliefs cannot be overemphasized.

It was never the function of public education to become thought and philosophy police for generations of Americans. However, in the NEA's effort to create a socialistic country, educators have waged a war to win the minds of children. Literate, self-sufficient people are a threat to socialism because they will not allow government to impinge on their freedoms by interfering in every facet of their private lives. Thus, with socialism its ultimate goal, the NEA has a vested interest in keeping American citizens illiterate—a nation of illiterates is no threat to a socialist government because most will lack the confidence and intelligence to challenge elitist authority. Public education must abort its mission to manipulate the minds of its students and return to its first and most basic responsibility: to teach reading, writing, and math skills. Indeed, if socialism is truly the best way to govern, an intelligent, literate society will determine that for themselves.

Endnotes

1. John Dewey, *Humanist Manifesto 1* (Buffalo, N.Y.: Prometheus Books), 3.

2. Charles L. Glen, "Religion and Public Education—Can We Stop the Fighting?" *The Reformed Journal*, vol. 34, no. 6: 12.

3. John D. McNeil, *Curriculum, A Comprehensive Introduction* (Boston: Little, Brown and Company, 1985), 4-5.

4. Samuel L. Blumenfeld, *NEA: Trojan Horse in American Education*, (Boise, Idaho: The Paradigm Company, 1984), 125.

5. Ibid., 130-31.

6. Ibid., 113.

7. *McGuffey's Third Eclectic Reader*, rev. ed. (New York: American Book Company, 1920), 74-75.

8. Jack Prelutsky, "The Sorceress," *Cross the Golden River*, Fourth Grade Student Project Book (Chicago: Harcourt, Brace, Jovanovich, 1986), 93.

9. "Impressions" series, Second Grade Teacher's Anthology (Chicago: Harcourt, Brace, Jovanovich, 1986), 114.

10. "Impressions" series, Fourth Grade Teacher's Anthology (Chicago: Harcourt, Brace, Jovanovich, 1986), 70.

11. Hebrews 11:1.

12. Blumenfeld, *Trojan Horse*, 57-62.

13. Ibid., 94.

14. McNeil, *Curriculum*, 33.

15. Blumenfeld, *Trojan Horse*, 57-62.

16. Ibid., 127.

17. Steven Marcus, *The New York Times Magazine* (6 November 1983): 84.

18. Blumenfeld, *Trojan Horse*, 128-30.

19. Ibid.

20. William F. Jasper, "Outcome-Based Education: Skinnerian Conditioning in the Classroom," *The New American* (23 August 1993): 5.

21. Ibid.

3

Goals 2000

On 31 March 1994, the Goals 2000: Educate America Act became law. The law will impact all 15,700 school districts and has been labeled a "massively intrusive bureaucratic nightmare." Goals 2000 creates more government through panels like the National Education Goals Panel, the National Education Standards and Improvement Council, and the National Skill Standards Board. These committees will set national "voluntary" standards for schools. Goals 2000 will invade every American home through mandatory Outcome-Based Education, and all the violations of personal privacy that implies. Further, government will keep detailed dossiers on every American child, *from the day he is born*. That information will be stored in the Elementary and Secondary Integrated Data System, enabling the state to keep a cumulative record of your child until the day he dies.

Government calls Goals 2000 a "lifelong learning" plan, but Bill Clinton was more telling when, before signing the bill into law, he referred to the essential role of the states as "laboratories of democracy" and gave his opinion that the education of our children "is and always has been a State responsibility."[1] Ann Herzer, a teacher and education writer, has been warning Americans about the dangers of OBE for years. She told *The New American* that "through OBE we are actually implementing the Soviet poly-technic system of education, and, incredibly, most conservative organizations and Christian groups that should be opposing it are completely oblivious to the threat." In making Goals 2000 law, government seized every parent's power to make decisions regarding educational reform and gave it to the state.

Of great concern is the fact that "most conservative organizations and Christian groups . . . are oblivious" to the dangers of this legislation. In questioning Christian educators who favor Goals 2000 (mandatory Outcome-Based Education), two things were sadly apparent: not one of them had read the entire legislation and all naively assumed that teachers administering the curriculum would have a Judeo-Christian value system.

The nationally mandated Goals 2000 is the same type of program the Chicago School District declared an abject failure. Over five years, they invested $7.5 million, only to find that their students were falling behind on standardized tests as a result of the very program that was alleged to be a "pacesetter for the nation." *Learning* magazine reported that many of Chicago's students were "entering high school . . . without ever having read a book and *without being able to read one*" (emphasis added).[2] It was further reported that seventy-five hundred of the total students enrolled, as assessed on the Tests of Academic Progress (TAP), scored at the tenth percentile—a score they could have achieved by simply answering the questions at random! About the same time that Chicago embarked on its OBE program, Washington, D.C. did the same—with the same tragic results.

Goals 2000 is the culmination of decades of careful planning by humanistically inspired educators such as John Dewey. Like Dewey's Laboratory School, Goals 2000 is designed to manipulate thought and de-emphasize the cognitive skills needed to learn reading, writing, and math. By using the same behavioral-adjustment techniques Dewey used, government hopes to restructure society and will use Goals 2000 curriculum to indoctrinate children in an effort to subordinate them to government. The intent of Goals 2000 is to shift allegiance from family and country and redirect it toward global citizenship and one world government. As former president Bush liked to say, "We're preparing youth for the New World Order."

The overall concept of the legislation is structured to include everyone, but the primary vehicle for Goals 2000 is public schools because children are the easiest to influence toward change. On page 37 of "America 2000," we are told that "if the United States is to maintain a strong and responsible democracy . . . all of our citizens must be involved in achieving these goals." In her in-depth work on the subject, Kathy Finnegan says that if all aspects of this law are implemented, "there is not a post-secondary institution, work place, or home where the tentacles of this government monstrosity will not reach."[3]

Under Goals 2000, the federal government determines national standards for school spending, creates uniform requirements for schools and class size, and dictates that curricula for all public schools must be "aligned to [Goals 2000] content standards." (Don't stop reading if your children attend private school; if government has its way, Goals 2000 will soon be mandated in *all* schools!) This legislation will affect all home-schooled children and all children enrolled in private schools because, soon, the American Achievement Tests (AAT) administered through Goals 2000 will be the standard for entrance to higher education and job markets. Though presented as "academic" tests, AATs have less to do with measuring literacy skills than they do with measuring philosophies; they are really designed to present government with a personality profile of your child. Nationally mandated curriculum is a violation of constitutional law, which has historically given individual states the right to choose their own curricula. So it's more than likely, that after AATs are administered, government will declare that students are not up to par. That will open the door for political "educrats" to blame the failure on a diversity of curricula and teaching methods throughout the nation. They will use their "concern" over that "crisis" to usher in the "need" for a uniform national curriculum.

Rhetoric suggests that participation in Goals 2000 is "voluntary" and "will maximize local control over education," but nothing could be further from the truth. Goals 2000 is *not voluntary*, and it undeniably usurps power from local governments. This legislation will eventually render moot the need for local school boards and school choice: What difference will it make what your community wants or where your child attends school if all schools are mandated to teach the same thing at the same time? Whether or not your district wants it, Goals 2000 is federal law that dictates Outcome-Based Education for everyone and demands that federal aid to elementary and secondary schools is "contingent upon each state's compliance with national goals and standards."[4] Under Title I, Goals 2000 provides "a framework for the reauthorization of *all* Federal education programs" (emphasis added).

Any state wanting federal funds must submit "standards" to the U.S. Department of Education explaining what children "are expected to know and do." If those standards do not meet the objectives of Goals 2000, and hence, produce "outcomes" pleasing to the state, funding can—*and most likely will*—be refused. Thus, we have government's definition of "voluntary" participation!

With Goals 2000, we can expect even less emphasis on academics and still more emphasis on philosophies as government uses the classroom to mold our children into dutiful servants of the state. For all but the academic elite, vocational training apprenticeships will replace higher education, as labor joins hands with public schools to create the perfect socialist utopia, right here in the good old U.S.A. We can already see this happening in inner-city schools all across America, as less emphasis is put on literacy skills and more opportunity is made available for teaching shop-type courses or "vocational skills."

Phyllis Schlafly, a longtime opponent of OBE, notes that supporters of the curriculum are "perfectly content to have . . . schools turn out quotas of semi-literate workers who can be trained to perform menial tasks under supervision." OBE proponents are content with "semi-literate workers" because most likely they will not question the authority or value of a socialized, one-world government. Those who disagree with Ms. Schlafly's statement must question how government could have any *other* motive? What advantage is there in prolonging the existence of a system of education that is failing to create literate citizens? If socialism is not the goal, what is it?

OBE proponents can continue to spin the rhetoric, but academic test scores do not lie! If the NEA wants to convince America that OBE is effective, why doesn't it raise the academic test standard to what it was in 1960 and issue the SAT as it existed then? Let parents judge for themselves the value of look-say reading methods and outcome-based education.

A Total Restructuring of Society

Under the guise of national educational reform, Goals 2000 aspires to completely "restructure society." Toward that end, it begins with a list of mandated, state-dictated outcomes, euphemistically called National Educational Goals (NEGs). On the surface, the goals seem admirable; what is frightening is the ideology behind these mandates and the government's plan for implementing them. If there was ever a line in the sand government couldn't cross, the foot of Goals 2000 has obliterated that line. This legislation is so insidiously deceptive that without studying it in-depth (which legislators seldom do) even the most astute observer would be hard-pressed to con-

ceive the evil behind it or the devastating effect it will
have on the American family and, ultimately, the nation.

When dealing with OBE, one of the first things one
learns is that words used to describe it must be carefully
dissected because they almost always have been given
new meaning. One can never take a statement about
OBE at face value.

Goal #1) Every child in America will start school ready
to learn.

Goal #2) The high school graduation rate will increase to 90 percent.

Goal #3) Students will leave grades four, eight, and
twelve having demonstrated competency in challenging
subject matter, including English, mathematics, history,
science, and geography; and every school in America will
ensure that all students learn to use their minds well, so
they may be prepared for responsible citizenship, further
learning, and productive employment in our modern
economy.

Goal #4) U.S. students will be first in the world in
science and mathematics achievement.

Goal #5) Every adult will be literate and will possess
the knowledge and skills necessary to compete in a global
economy and exercise the rights and responsibilities of
citizenship.

Goal #6) Every school in America will be free of drugs
and violence and will offer a disciplined environment
conducive to learning.

Goal #7) By the year 2000, every school will promote
partnerships that will increase parental involvement and
participation in promoting the social, emotional, and academic growth of children.

Individually, each mandate is admirable and desirable. But, when one studies the government's plan for
implementing those mandates, it becomes painfully obvious that the state has motives quite different from what
the goals imply.

Examining Goals #1 and #7

Scrutiny of the mandates reveals that, in order to comply with Goal #1, "American homes must be places of learning," and "parents should have access to the support and training required to fulfill this role." Goals 2000 does not define what "a place of learning" is, nor does it admit that parents will "gain access to support and training" by having a government agent forced into their home! In order to implement Goal #1—which, on the surface, seems in the best interest of every child—Goals 2000 purports to use programs like Parents as Teachers (PAT), so Goal #7 was added by the Clintons and accompanied by a request for additional funds for more PAT programs.

Parents as Teachers is a euphemism and does not mean involvement by the biological parent! PAT programs mean the intrusion of state-appointed "parent educators," defined in H.R. 520 as persons "hired by the . . . State . . . to administer group meetings, home visits and developmental screening." In other words, the state assumes the right to tell parents how to raise their children.

While enrolled in PAT programs, parents must attend a minimum of four group meetings and agree to eight home visits per year. Supposedly, this allows the state time to evaluate the parent and determine whether or not his or her parenting skills are adequate for the child to remain in the home. Should the "parent educator" deem the parent's skills insufficient, the state then has a legal right to take the child from his parents. According to Bettina Dobbs, former consultant to the U.S. Department of Health, PAT programs "will result in state control of the children and reduce parents to the status of breeders and supervised custodians."[5] Alarmingly, over two hundred PAT programs are currently in place in forty states, though not all go by the same name. And, if passed, H.R. 520 will even provide funding for PAT programs that target expectant mothers. It's not enough that government agents are invading our homes, they want to impose themselves on our children before they're even born! (Isn't it interesting that government has such a keen interest in the "welfare" of the same children they allow to be butchered in the womb?)

Under the deceptive pretense of "educational screening," both parents and children are scrutinized and evaluated by the state. According to the U.S. Advisory Board on Child Abuse, the purpose of programs like PAT is to identify families where a potential for child abuse exists. In reality, when these programs are implemented, the government becomes the guest that wouldn't leave. Once inside the home, the state abuses its privilege and assumes rights never intended by the hosts. PAT—and other programs like it—gives government the right to impose itself upon the family, making "suggestions" about everything (literally!) from how to arrange the furniture to how to solve personal problems. It is not unusual for parents who reject the state's "suggestions" to be negatively reviewed by the state's agent—an outcome which often has devastating effects on the family.

Parents are seldom told that children participating in PAT (or similar) programs are given personal computer code numbers, which government will use to track their every move. Computerized data banks will store information about the child's health and academic achievement, as well as personal information gleaned from the "assessment tests" each child will be forced to take in public school. The state will use those tests to gain information about what parents do for a living, how many siblings a child has, and whether or not he attends church. Should your child get a teacher who doesn't like him and, thus, attaches a defamatory label alongside his name, that label will follow him throughout his academic career.

Of dire concern is the fact that the computer used to code all children assumes that every child is mentally ill; there is no code for "normal!" (Thus, all children can be generally classified "at risk," a designation that allows the

NEA to collect millions of additional tax dollars, annually.) The theory of "mass mental illness" was first explained in 1973 during a speech given to a group of two thousand teachers who had gathered in Denver, Colorado, for a conference. Harvard University professor Pierce told the group that every child in America "is mentally ill, because he comes to school with allegiance toward . . . our founding fathers . . . , the preservation of this form of government, patriotism, nationalism, sovereignty. . . . All of that proves *the children are sick*" (emphasis added). Accepting Pierce's logic, the next step was for government to change the "allegiances" of children by altering the parent-child relationship. They are attempting to do this through programs like PAT, where state agents (Change Agents or state-certified public educators) will step in to "parent" the child. Ironically, the programs needed to implement such radical change are all paid for with tax dollars, hard-earned by the very citizens the state seeks to subordinate!

Because government must have a reason to intrude in the personal lives of its citizens, the "at-risk" designation was invented so government agents could get a foot inside your door. A list of "at-risk" designations follows, as noted in the Revised Risk Factor Form. An "at-risk" family includes any family with one or more of the following problems:

• premature babies, or babies delivered in emergency or birth trauma situations,

• children exhibiting slow growth, poor appetites, or frequent illnesses,

• any parent unable "to cope with inappropriate child behavior"; this includes "spanking" as discipline, and "inconsistency,"

• any parent who is ill, overweight, tired, depressed, handicapped, injured, or appears to be of "low-level intelligence,"

• overindulgence or "undue spoiling" on the part of the parent,

• stress (due to a parent who travels frequently, moving, death in the family, divorce or separation, birth of a sibling, job loss, or change, etc., etc., etc.).

That pretty much includes every human being on the face of the earth, but lest Big Brother forget anyone, an "other" category was created that cautions "parent-educators" (state agents) to look for such "at-risk" tendencies as allergies, cigarette smoking in the house, family history of hearing loss, and "lack of stimulation" or "*over*-stimulation" in the toys our children play with![6]

PAT guidelines allow the agent to determine whether or not a parent is "healthy" enough to raise a child, even though that agent may see the parent only once. Further, we don't know whose definition of "healthy" the evaluator is using—does a bad cold render a parent too unhealthy to raise his or her own children? How about cancer? Does the state mean physical health or mental health? Is PMS a mental illness? What about overeating? No one knows because the state's definition is so purposely vague.

Equally disturbing is the fact that such a determination is left to a government agent who may or may not be having a *bad hair day!* What if a Christian family is assigned a "parent educator" who happens to be an atheist and, therefore, considers that having a Bible in the home places your child "at risk"? Certainly, biblical values are not in accordance with the socialistic movement in this country. Or, what if the state agent happens to "visit" just minutes after your five-year-old has been spanked for throwing his sister's retainer into the toilet? The reality exists that, if your family gets a state agent who doesn't like something about you, the agent can manipulate the law to say whatever he wants it to say.

PAT and other home visitation programs are intrusive, at best; and there are cases where such programs have caused children to be temporarily removed from the home. It's impossible to measure the devastation that false accusations have caused individual families even though the children are returned. Children are emotionally traumatized, marriages break up as a result of the stress, and jobs are often lost. Legal fees have forced families into financial ruin, as parents were forced to defend themselves in court for the *right* to raise their own children. Every day reputations are being destroyed, and individuals are irreparably damaged as government further imposes itself upon the family.

If you think the PAT program sounds ridiculous and that it will never happen in the United States of America or in your lifetime—it's happening now!

Examining Goal #2

Who could argue the merit of increasing the graduation rate to 90 percent? However, given the track record of the NEA and the declining literacy rate due to OBE curriculum, it's almost laughable to think government can achieve this goal. However, even as a skeptic, I will admit it *is* possible for Goals 2000 to hit this mark—if they continue to lower academic standards and use a national test designed by the president of the NEA.

Examining Goal #3

Certainly, every parent wants his child to be able to "demonstrate competency" in English, mathematics, history, science, and geography, and to "use his mind well." But, many parents do *not* want the academic subjects taught infused with humanistic ideologies and psychological techniques designed to alter the child's belief system. Indeed, parents are biblically mandated to "train up" their own children according to God's principles. For government to impose humanistic philosophies upon public school children is as wrong as government forcing an atheist to attend a Christian school—as if that would ever happen! Goals 2000 pollutes education by mixing adulterated philosophies with pure academics.

The intrusive American Achievement Test, which will determine who "demonstrates competency" and who does not, is based more on what students think philosophically than on what they know academically. In other words, if your child agrees with government-dictated "outcomes" in the subjects tested, he will pass. If he philosophically disagrees, he will be "remediated." (That's statespeak; it means he'll fail.)

Examining Goal #4

As the only remaining "super power" in the world, it stands to reason that our children should "be the first in the world in science and mathematics achievement." Thankfully, the National Council of Teachers of Mathematics and the Mathematical Sciences Education Board have defined (in Goal #4) "what all students must know . . . in order to be mathematically competent." We can all sleep better at night knowing that there are educrats out there willing to spend their time determining "what we should know."

In all its pomposity, Goals 2000 fails to provide a single strategy for achieving this goal, or teaching "what we need to know"; and so, as Ms. Finnegan points out, "the only way we're likely to be tops by the year 2000 is if Korea, Japan, etc., deliberately 'dumb-down' their curricula as we have done."[7]

Examining Goal #5

Adults will be lured into the web of Goals 2000 through mandatory PAT and Lifelong Learning programs which will require that they undergo continuous training and recertification for jobs. In order for adults to "possess the knowledge and skills necessary to compete in a global economy," (note the buzzword "global" economy) and "exercise the rights and responsibilities of citizenship," the government now feels that parenting and relationship skills should be taught to every adult! They say we need to become better "parents, neighbors, citizens, and friends!"

On page 23 of "America [Goals] 2000," we are told that, as adults in the new America, we must "make a life." Goals 2000 then sets out to create a strategy whereby adults will be able to meet that goal: "Business and labor will be asked to adopt a strategy to establish job-related . . . skill standards, built around core proficiencies, and to develop skill certificates to accompany these standards." Can you imagine? Picture yourself, in front of your co-workers, shaking your boss's hand as you proudly accept your "skill certificate" for "Most Proficient Friend." And, what if you don't get the skill certificate? Will you be demoted or refused a promotion?

This is not science fiction; this is the law of the land—this is Goals 2000!

Apparently, the secretaries of education and labor have been assigned the task of developing "voluntary standards for all industries." What happens when those "voluntary" standards become "mandated"? Who will do the paper work? Who will be delegated the responsibility of determining who meets the core proficiency standards and who fails? And, what will be the fate of those who fail?

Under this ludicrous law, Goals 2000 proposes to create "skill clinics" in every large community and worksite (more government, requiring more taxes). Through these clinics, state agents will allegedly tell us "what we know, don't know, and need to know" and will assess our "living skills" at the same time they assess our skills in job-related areas. Undoubtedly, government will then deem itself qualified to make recommendations to our employers.

The last objective listed under this goal is to increase "the proportion of college graduates who demonstrate an advanced ability to think critically." In other words, if Goals 2000 is a success, we can expect a much higher percentage of students graduating from college with "politically correct" attitudes and sympathy toward a *socialist* form of government.

Examining Goal #6

Citing the problems of drugs and violence, Goal #6 dictates that "every school district will develop a comprehensive K-12 drug and alcohol prevention education program" and that "drug and alcohol curriculum should be taught as an integral part of health education." That sounds like an admirable goal. What they don't admit is that countless studies prove that drug prevention programs, when taught within the context of "values-neutral" curricula consistent with OBE, actually increase drug use among students.

Values-neutral curriculum dictates that students teach themselves; they are told *they* must determine what is right and wrong through experience. Considering the elements of immaturity and natural curiosity, mixed with values-neutral ideology, one can see why preteen and teenaged children would reason that "they can't know for sure" if drugs are wrong for them unless they experiment. On the one hand, children are told to create a value system; on the other, they are told that nothing is absolutely right or wrong. This is extremely confusing to children who *need* guidance. (It also begs the question: If everything is relative, why is a value system important at all?) By eliminating moral absolutes and teaching children that they have a right to complete autonomy, public education devalues church and parental authority and places the child in the position of becoming his own teacher. Encouraging children to "experience life" and "make their own determinations, based on what feels right" makes about as much sense as placing a loaded pistol on the coffee table and telling your six-year-old not to touch it after you leave the room: He's going to pick up the gun, there's no doubt about it; he may kill himself, or he may not.

Why should we believe government will give us schools "free of violence" when they won't even keep the most savage criminals off the streets long enough to complete a jail sentence? How much will a child fear punishment when minors are committing heinous crimes every day and walking out of courthouses free? Regardless of what Goals 2000 promises, that's the reality we all know, and that's what the criminals of the future know because they see the result of our court system in action every day! Consider the audacity of a government mandate that promises freedom from violence, with our present system the prototype for success.

It's absolutely absurd for a government that denies the existence of moral absolutes to promise "a disciplined environment conducive to learning." If, as values-neutral curriculum claims, any behavior is acceptable, then no behavior can be considered "wrong." Thus, no behavior can be "disciplined." The only way to stop violence and abuse of any kind is to teach our children that moral absolutes *do* exist, and certain behaviors *are* wrong!

Be an America 2000 Community!

Under the government's plan, individual communities can apply for elite designation as an "America 2000 Community" if they agree to 1) adopt all seven goals, 2) develop a community-wide strategy to achieve them, 3) design a means to measure results, and 4) plan for and support a "New American School."

New American Schools are completely experimental, but Goals 2000 plans to use your tax dollars and mine to build 535 of them by 1996. Government says, that in the New American Schools, "time, space, staffing and other resources . . . may be used in ways yet to be imagined." (We can only hope they're "imagined" before the students arrive on the first day of class!) Some of the New American schools "may make extensive use of computers, distance learning, interactive videodiscs (virtual reality),

and other modern tools," and some "may radically alter
the customary modes of teaching and learning," while we
all pay for it.

Where Are the Parents?

Proponents say that Goals 2000 will empower parents
to direct their children's education, but, again, nothing
could be further from the truth. Government wants to *be*
your child's parent. As we've seen with PAT programs,
"parental involvement," as defined and implemented
through Goals 2000, is quite different from anything most
parents imagine. In reality, Goals 2000 purports to inte-
grate more and more social services into the public school
system, thus subordinating parental rights to the state
and involving government even more intrusively in our
private lives. The same government that says it wants
parents "involved" assumes the right to give our minor
children birth control without our knowledge or consent
and has mandated that public schools force a radical
homosexual agenda on innocent children against the loud
protests of their parents.

Regardless of what Goals 2000 says, the *reality* is that
parents, en masse, have called for a departure from OBE
and a return to cognitive learning and traditional academics. Meanwhile, our government, which claims to
"care" so deeply and assumes to know what's best for
everyone, ignored the majority and responded by passing
the Goals 2000 legislation, mandating the very thing the
majority of parents oppose. One thing is certain, we must
never listen to what government *says*; we must scrutinize
everything government *does*.

It's absurd to believe that government will allow parents to be more involved in education when they're teaching students that freedom from parental authority is the
utopian ideal of the society the state seeks to create! (If
you believe they want you involved, try getting a copy of

the assessment test they're giving your child, and see how far you get.) What most young adults of today cannot see is that if they don't take the state's intrusion seriously and contend for their constitutional rights now, if they don't rise up to defend themselves against the government's involvement in every area of public and private life, they will be raising their own children in a one-world socialist state.

In the true spirit of socialism, educational reformers are quick to laud the benefit of "village commons" on public school grounds where social, health, and psychological services are offered regardless of the recipient's ability to pay. Such radical and costly intervention by government further impairs public education's ability to teach by forcing school districts to provide services they're not qualified (or financially able) to provide. If current trends persist, every public school campus will become a Center for Social Services, offering psychological counseling, job placement, drug intervention programs, welfare, parenting classes, and school-based health clinics for contraceptive distribution. There is no question that some health services are needed, but there is much debate as to whether or not such services should coexist with education on the public school campus. Don't schools have enough to do? With an estimated forty million functionally illiterate Americans, isn't it logical to use tax dollars allocated for education on education?

The Curriculum

"Transformational" OBE involves using a new curriculum specifically designed to bring about radical change. The curriculum is "affective"—instead of teaching facts, it uses manipulative means to change feelings and attitudes. Goals set in transformational OBE are often aimed at altering a child's value system, usually questioning the child's views about sexual behavior—always steering the student away from traditional biblical morality toward an acceptance of deviant sexual behavior as "normal." This explains the push for prohomosexual curriculum in the elementary school classroom.

Cognitive skills are not completely abandoned within the context of OBE, but, when used, the exercises almost always deal with the subjective. For example, instead of studying the U.S. Constitution as it was written and then being tested on what they know, students may be encouraged to write a new constitution. Children may be asked to write a paper on the origin of man, and that certainly requires some cognitive thought; but, as happened with a young person I know, if they question Darwin's theory of evolution and suggest divine creation, they may fail the assignment because their essay "does not project the proper outcome." (This student was told she "had an 'A' paper, but an 'F' idea!" She refused to rewrite her essay and gratefully accepted the "F," getting full support from her parents.)

Goals 2000 curriculum places exhaustive emphasis on each student's social, philosophical, and emotional development and spends 40-50 percent *less* class time on cognitive (reasoning) skills. The architects of Goals 2000 curriculum assume that subjects like "attitude adjustment," "self-esteem," and "affective learning behaviors" are more important than reading, writing, and math; the state is more interested in what children think and feel than it is in their ability to write or articulate those thoughts in a literate manner. By virtue of the way this curriculum is administered, government has assumed the right to know your child's most personal thoughts; that way, if your child's opinion is opposed to the state's, the Department of Education can step in and adjust his attitude.

The entire premise of OBE is to manipulate children's minds until they conform to the philosophy of those doing the manipulating—in this case, the state. Instead of teaching the independence of spirit and thought that made

America great, OBE restricts independent thought and encourages interdependence upon government. Instead of rewarding diligence and hard work, OBE discourages both by promoting outcome-based programs that have the same results for everyone. Motivation, and the enthusiasm that competition inspires, is lost as educrats seek to create a lethargic, automated society which will be content with government directing its life.

OBE removes the incentive for excellence, making public schools institutes for mediocrity. Individual achievement and healthy competition are discouraged in place of "cooperative learning," where students may only advance in groups. Though your child may be the brightest, he will not advance until the other members of his class "master the stated behavioral goals." Students are no longer responsible for their own success or failure; instead, "programs are developed, tried on a sample of . . . learners, and revised until the program attains intended results."[8] In other words, students will be taught the same philosophies repeatedly until everyone agrees. If that sounds like brainwashing, it is! In addition, test standards will continually be lowered until enough students pass to make the curriculum appear successful. Declining achievement scores, dull textbooks, dropping enrollment, and weakened graduation requirements are the result of a curriculum that places more importance on attitudes than academics.

Defining Curricula

The NEA insists that a return to traditional academics is occurring, but, once again, we must look closely at definitions. According to the NEA, a child must "meet academic requirements in five areas: literature and the arts, [new] history, social analysis and moral reasoning, science, and foreign cultures."[9] Reading and math skills are not mentioned. "Social analysis and moral reasoning" means values-clarification. "Science" means sex education and prohomosexual curriculum, and "foreign cultures" means cultural pluralism. Because all subjects are taught using OBE methods, the few academic courses mentioned must be altered to fit the curriculum. For example, when studying history, "each student compiles his or her own version of a historical event."

Most parents would not object to their children studying the facts, as recorded by qualified, unbiased historians, and then analyzing a historical event from different perspectives. However, in "New History," students do not necessarily study the facts at all. Instead, they're encouraged to recreate history with outcome-based goals as the objective. It doesn't matter to the NEA if the facts are lost while translating history into the language of political correctness. In fact, it's advantageous (for the advancement of socialism) to ignore the facts altogether; one directive of OBE is to change the way children *feel* about America's form of government. In the interest of ethical pluralism and a long-range globalist agenda, the NEA wants to make ethnic students feel better about themselves while making American students feel guilty about the way their ancestors treated minorities. The NEA claims to "interpret [history] from different points of view,"[10] but what it actually does is misrepresent and alter the facts surrounding historical events. Thus, we have the NEA's definition of "traditional academics."

Not surprisingly, a study by the U.S. Department of Education revealed that "those responsible for [creating textbooks] appear to have a deep-seated fear of any form of . . . contemporary Christianity. . . . This fear has led the authors to deny and repress the importance of this kind of religion in American life. . . . It is common in [text] books to treat Thanksgiving without explaining to whom the Pilgrims gave thanks. . . . No mention is made of God."[11]

"Look, Ma: No Grades!"

Some students are more intelligent than others. They will do better in school because they have higher IQs and better memory retention than their classmates. Some students are more competitive than others, and they will do better in school than those who are less motivated because they try harder. An "A" has always been the achiever's reward for diligence and hard work; an "F" has always signified a need to try harder. The comparative grading system has always promoted a healthy competitiveness and given children an incentive to achieve and is an accurate way for teachers to measure progress. Honor rolls and valedictorian honors have always been a tradition, as students are recognized for outstanding academic achievement. Now that Goals 2000 is law, the comparative grading system—always an impetus to serious students—will become a thing of the past.[12] "Carnegie Units," traditionally used to measure credits required in academic subjects, are being replaced with "learning outcomes" that cannot be measured on a grading scale; for the most part, they are subjective determinations regarding the way a child thinks, not what he knows. Consequently, one either "passes" (because he produces the right outcome and agrees with the state) or "fails" (because he has an opinion of his own, opposed to the state's).

According to William Spady, a leading OBE proponent and director of the International Center on Outcome-Based Restructuring, there is no room for comparative grading in Outcome-Based Education. Mr. "Success-For-*All*-Students-And-Staff" Spady says, "grades only invalidate students"; he wants everyone to succeed so everyone "feels good" and is "validated," even if the only way to achieve success for all is to lower the standard for everyone. Even to an obsolete cognitive thinker like myself, the absurdity of Spady's "logic" defies understanding. If pseudo-intellectuals like Spady have their way,

America will soon be a nation of validated, albeit illiterate and unemployable, citizens!

Teachers are quick to point out that traditional grading methods have their problems too. "Sometimes," one teacher said, "kids can be tracked into certain groups at an early age because of a grade, and be unable to move ahead because he thinks he will never be able to learn in a higher group. . . . They're given names like 'turtles' for slower kids, and 'rabbits' for the more advanced—in elementary school, especially." Certainly, the point is worthy of consideration; no system is perfect. But, when considering the OBE alternative, how does the individual student benefit from being in a class where everyone is required to know exactly the same thing at the same time? How does such a system encourage competition or inspire creativity? How can such a mundane method of brainwashing be intellectually stimulating or challenging?

"A" Is for Assessment Test

Now that OBE is federal law, "assessment testing" will be used to introduce curricula into the schools. Your child will be given a "pretest" to determine his attitudes on specific subjects like the environment, global citizenship, ethical pluralism, and diversity of family situations. After the pretest, he will be served "learning nuggets," carefully prepared to brainwash him into responding "correctly" to the issues presented. Following the nugget sessions, your child will be given a reassessment test to see if he (finally) understands the "correct" responses. What follows next should really boil your blood: If your child fails to give the response the state desires, he will be "remediated," which is a euphemistic way of saying that he will be held back so government can continue to retest (brainwash) him until he gives the state's response. Children failing to respond according to the state's mandate will be "refused acceleration to the next learning level" until they get the message.

In order to illustrate what assessment testing is, examine the following test question, cited by Dr. Wayne Sedlak in his OBE Position Paper, Volume I. The example comes from an actual test administered by the Carnegie Foundation for the Advancement of Teaching and is indicative of what you can expect from OBE assessment tests across the nation:

> There is a secret club at school called the Midnight Artists.
>
> They go out late at night and paint funny sayings and pictures on buildings. A student is asked to join the club. In this situation, I would join the club when I knew:
>
> (a) My best friend asked me to join
>
> (b) the most popular students were in the club
>
> (c) my parents would ground me if they found out I joined

Note the following: First of all, it's assumed that the child *will* join the club; the decision *not* to join is not an option. Second, because refusal to join is not an option, the question assumes that the child is willing to break the law by vandalizing property. Third, failure to offer a chance to opt out of committing the crime implies that there's nothing wrong with spray-painting other people's property. The question also encourages obstinance when it suggests that a child would join the club simply because his parents wouldn't like it. (How many children do you think "got an idea" to start such a club after taking the test?)

If your child happens to recognize that "painting funny sayings and pictures on buildings" is wrong and, thus, chooses *none* of the options, he will be marked "incorrect." Enough "incorrects" after similar questions, and he "fails to advance to the next learning level." Apart from the fact that such questions are a clear invasion of your child's privacy, they have nothing to do with literacy concepts. And, as you might expect, the state's response to moral and ethical questions may differ greatly from your own. For example, how do you feel about sex outside of marriage? Do you want a government that mandates sex education in kindergarten telling your child how he should think about sex? How do you feel about taking a human life? Is it all right with you if a government which legally allows tiny babies to be murdered in the womb imposes its view on your children? How do you feel about "global citizenship" and one-world government? Homosexuality?

Tests for younger children deliver the same message in a different envelope. For example, one grade school assessment test asks the question: "Which ONE of these is not a family?" Following the question is a picture of a traditional family, a picture of a soccer team, and a picture of two women and a child.

Think Right and Graduate

The socialistic premise upon which OBE was established deems parents ill-equipped to guide their own children and seeks to destroy the traditional family by separating our sons and daughters from parental authority and pointing them toward the collective authority of government. The only way a child can graduate from an OBE curriculum is to demonstrate the *correct* attitude, as determined and defined by the federal government through its Department of Education, and assessed by teachers subjectively. Refusal to agree with the state's position on any one of a myriad of issues could result in your child being denied a diploma! Equally as outrageous, employers will soon be required to seek resumés from schools for job applicants. Most likely, those resumés will come from the Elementary and Secondary Integrated Data System which will computer-code all little Americans in the future and keep a running account of their "attitudes" from the day they enter the public school system. That same computer will track your child's academic progress, record his personal beliefs and values, his family history, and his medical and health records. In other words, whenever your child sneezes, the government will know.

Individual OBE Plans

Soon, all school districts will use OBE curricula, but government has been gracious enough to allow them to select from several, and even to create their own curriculum as long as their projected "outcomes" are in agreement with the state's.

Direction 2000 was Littleton, Colorado's OBE plan. In 1993, a brochure described their desired curriculum for the future by listing thirteen "Integrated Learning Outcomes" in which students "must demonstrate quality." The school board in Littleton determined that their children should be proficient in the subjects of "self-estimate, reflection and thoughtfulness, perspective and humor, tolerance, stress management, empathizing, creative thinking, personal goal setting, self-respect, and conflict management and resolution." Uh . . . what about reading? What about English? What about arithmetic? Biology?

As enhancement to their Integrated Learning Outcomes, the Littleton school district issued the following statement: "As well as academics, teachers will be expected to help students develop a personal set of values." (What if your child's teacher happens to have values completely different from those you teach in the home? What if the teacher is sexually promiscuous? Homosexual? A member of a cult?)

Thankfully, some astute Colorado parents recalled a time when it was considered appropriate for parents and churches to teach ethics and morality to their children, and they took action against the school board that adopted the curriculum. Three "back to basics" candidates competed for positions on the board, and all three were *elected*. Securing a majority on the five-member board, conservatives issued a moratorium on the development of performance outcomes for students and were in the process of reinstituting traditional graduation requirements when the Clinton administration signed Goals 2000 into law. Given that all fifteen elementary principals within Littleton's district favored OBE curriculum, this was a significant victory for the parents. The Littleton victory serves well to demonstrate parental opposition to OBE curriculum.[13] If Goals 2000 is met with such firm opposition, government will be forced to reverse itself.

The Cost of Failure

As cited in the beginning of this chapter, the citizens of Chicago spent $7.5 million over five years before abandoning OBE because they determined that their children suffered academically because of it. Littleton, Colorado, spent $1,270,500 to implement its OBE program before they were forced to abandon the curriculum due to the loud outcry of parents. Similar scenarios have been repeated across the nation, with parents strongly objecting to the ideology behind OBE and the immeasurable cost to taxpayers.

To deem OBE a success or failure depends, of course, upon one's definition of each term. Indeed, that which conservative Christians view as "failure," will almost always be deemed "successful" by those with a humanist world view and a socialistic bent. One of those who declares OBE successful is Harvard professor Anthony Oettinger who also said, "Teaching reading and writing is probably a waste of time, anyway." He then goes on to speculate as to the value of literacy at all, suggesting that what's really important is to "help citizens function well in society."

Now that OBE is required in order for states to receive government funding for educational programs, extensive teacher retraining will be required in all districts, and taxpayers are expected (once again) to pick up the tab.

Parental Rights Restoration Amendment

In 1978, Congress passed a Protection of Pupil Rights Amendment (PPRA) which prohibited schools from imposing psychological or psychiatric tests or treatment on children, or from requiring them to answer personal questions about sex, attitudes, or family beliefs or matters, which might be considered an invasion of privacy. The law was largely ignored until 1984 when public demand forced the U.S. Department of Education to issue regulations regarding the legislation.

In response to the obvious intrusiveness of assessment testing relative to Goals 2000, Sen. Chuck Grassley (R-Iowa) created new legislation that simplifies the application of the PPRA. The NEA, and other school associations, stood in loud opposition to Grassley, who emerged victorious. Now, assessment tests, which ask personal and/or psychological questions, cannot be administered without prior written parental consent.

Parents must be informed regarding assessment testing, and they must initiate their right to see and study the tests their children are being given. Parents *do* have rights, but only if they claim those rights. Some schools will use every method possible to discourage parents from asserting their rights under the law. Parents must stand firm and not be discouraged. Schools are notorious for responding to requests for information by sending parents form letters which state that PPRA does not apply to the curriculum being challenged. Parents must stand their ground—PPRA applies to *all* curricula! If administrators refuse to give you the test, get legal representation if necessary. You have a legal right to this information, and you must not allow anyone to deny you the right to have it. If you meet opposition, remind the one refusing you the information that schools which do not comply with the Grassley Amendment risk losing federal funds.

The Grassley Amendment applies to "any survey, analysis or evaluation" that reveals private information, whether or not it meets some narrow definition of "psy-chological" or "psychiatric" testing. Simply, the amend-ment requires that if a test or questionnaire reveals pri-vate information, the school must get prior, written, pa-rental consent.[14]

Parents must stay informed; they must call the school and ask to see the assessment test *before* it is administered. Failure to cooperate almost certainly means that the test is intrusive and, probably, illegal. If you can't see the test before it's given, most states allow parents to see it after-ward. (There are always ways to secure copies of assess-ment tests if parents want them badly enough.) If an assessment test violates the Grassley Amendment and was administered without permission, parents must immedi-ately invoke their rights under the law and hold the school accountable. If enough parents take appropriate action, at the very least, it will be extremely difficult for the state to force the Goals 2000 agenda on the free citizens of America. At most, Goals 2000 will go down in flames!

Endnotes

1. Rhonda N. Smith, "Goals 2000 Heaps More Bureaucracy and Red Tape on Already Top-Heavy System," *Family Research Council Alert* (Washington, D.C.).

2. William F. Jasper, "Outcome-Based Education Skinnerian Conditioning in the Classroom," *The New American* (23 August 1993): 3.

3. Kathy Finnegan, "A Commentary on Goal 2000" as cited in James R. Patrick's *Research Manual America 2000/Goals 2000 Moving the Nation Educationally to a New World Order*, (Citizens for Excellence in Education, 1992), 3.

4. *Congressional Quarterly* (11 September 1993).

5. Kathi Hudson, *Reinventing America's Schools*, vol. 1, (NACE/ CEE, Box 3200, Costa Mesa, CA), 68.

6. Hudson, *Reinventing America's Schools* (NACE/CEE, 1992), 69-70.

7. Patrick, *Research Manual*, 10.

8. John D. McNeil, *Curriculum, A Comprehensive Introduction*, (Boston: Little, Brown and Company, 1985), 47.

9. Ibid., 66.

10. Ibid.

11. Paul Vitz, "Religion and Traditional Values in Public School Textbooks," *Education Newsline* (December 1985): 2.

12. Robert Slavin, "Mastery Learning Reconsidered" (Johns Hopkins University, 1987), as cited in *Outcome-Based Education Report #20*, from NACE/CCE, Costa Mesa, CA.

13. *Education Newsline* (March/April 1994): 4.

14. "Sen. Grassley Wins Victory for Parental Rights," *Education Reporter* (April 1994): 1.

4

The Homosexual Agenda

Do not lie with a man as one lies with a woman; that is detestable.

—Leviticus 18:22

They're targeting children at a very vulnerable point in their life. Kids are actually believing that it's okay to be this way and to act this way. It happened with me. I'm a pure example of that fact, and my concern is for all the other kids.
—Seventeen-year-old Marc Shelton, former homosexual, HIV positive, speaking of homosexual activists

Apart from the issue of morality, the AIDS epidemic demands that we use common sense when considering the homosexual lifestyle and that we evaluate it from a public safety perspective. Political agendas and religious philosophies aside, both heterosexuals and homosexuals must be practical and consider whether or not it's prudent to condone a lifestyle (or continue in one) that places ourselves, our loved ones, and our entire nation at risk.

The vast majority of those who accept homosexuality do so based on information received from the liberal media. Apart from what they hear and see on television, few people give much serious thought to the actual facts surrounding the homosexual lifestyle. Research reveals far more about the sexual perversities of homosexuals than most people want to know. The ways in which homosexuals allow themselves to be abused and humiliated in order to sexually satisfy themselves and their partners is a profoundly sad commentary on the lifestyle they have chosen. The actual practices of homosexuals, while incomprehensible to most people, do much to explain the psychological illness in that community. Resources are available that give specific details regarding those deviancies, but, apart from sensationalism, it would serve no purpose to give those details here.

The media constantly seeks ways to normalize homosexuality. Even home-decorating magazines like to feature the homes of homosexual couples, sometimes shown with their arms around each other. We see homosexuals on news footage, kissing or walking happily hand-in-hand. We're supposed to feel sympathetic as we read of their emotional trauma as they fight in court for the right to marry and raise children and be treated just like everyone else. Daily, we read of inequities allegedly done to homosexuals, as we are asked to support pending legislations which will give them special rights. But, we never read anything about what homosexuals actually do. That's because members of that community struggle to keep knowledge of their sexual practices secret because they know the information would repulse the vast majority of people. Activists realize that if the public knew the truth, we would never consider homosexuals "just like everyone else," nor would we ever view that lifestyle as "acceptable" because, clearly, it is not acceptable to most people.

Homosexuals prefer that the general population view them with indifference; that way, they can be left alone to get on with their business of taking over America, as described in an article in the homosexual magazine *Guide* in November 1987. The article, titled "The Overhauling of Straight America," instructs readers to "desensitize the public" so they'll "view homosexuality with indifference instead of . . . emotion." The authors encourage the media to portray homosexuals as "victims in need of protection so that straights will be inclined . . . to assume [that] role." The authors went on to chart a course to further advance the homosexual movement: "Make antidiscrimination the theme, and make the 'victimizers' look bad." Thus, the term *homophobe* was sown and cultivated. The authors said, "The public should be shown images of ranting homophobes. . . . These images might include the Ku Klux Klan demanding that gays be burned alive or castrated." Given the content of the *Guide* article, we can see that the media's portrayal of homosexuals as nice, "ordinary" people being persecuted for simply living their lives is no accident; the media has been well directed and has willingly complied, allowing itself to be manipulated by a very small minority of people.

Homosexual activists are the motivating force behind "political correctness"—the political double-speak that reclassified promiscuity, placing it in the category of an "alternate lifestyle," and now calls sexual perversion "sexual orientation." In a further effort to win public sympathy, activists continually identify themselves with historically oppressed people, who have no control over their skin color or place of birth. Equating homosexuals with ethnic minorities is as absurd as equating drug abusers with prostate cancer patients. In both cases, the former group makes a choice, while the latter has no control over their circumstance.

Early activists didn't like the word *homosexual* because God says He "detests" the practice of homosexuality, so the homosexual lobby put pressure on the media to call them "gay"—a term they felt projected a positive image. Homosexuals crave acceptance, and society unwittingly gives it to them by using the "gay" euphemism, which makes homosexuality sound like something it's not. So powerful is the homosexual movement that they have actually convinced the *New York Times*, the *Washington*

Post, and other major publications to print lists of phrases the media may and may not use when referring to them.

Those who do their research and then rationally consider all the implications of homosexuality seldom, if ever, endorse it. This author will not refer to homosexuals as "gay" because nothing about that lifestyle is gay, according to Webster's definition of that word. On the contrary, as much as the homosexual community wants us to think they're happy and "just like everyone else," countless psychological, medical, and sociological studies prove that the exact opposite is true.

Enrique Rueda was commissioned by the Free Congress Research and Education Foundation to write a comprehensive, unbiased study on homosexuality. The result of his research was a book titled *The Homosexual Network: Private Lives and Public Policy*. In his book, Rueda concludes that "when [the homosexual] subculture is examined in its own terms . . . it can only be described as a sick component of American society."[1] Rueda goes on to say that a goal of the homosexual movement is to influence public consciousness until homosexuality is accepted as the *norm*. Homosexuals plan to achieve their goal by continuing to expose the public to homosexuality in the media and to confuse the roles of men and women within the family—getting more than enough help from militant feminist organizations (almost always founded by lesbians) and Planned Parenthood, which is clearly on a mission to destroy the traditional family. The redefinition—and ultimate destruction of the family—is imperative to the success of the homosexual movement. Thus, activists are working from within to reorganize our legal and educational systems in order to advance that agenda.

In the field of education, homosexuals have an interest in Outcome-Based Education because it denies moral absolutes and endorses the acceptance of homosexuality. In the government arena, homosexuals are expanding their efforts to pass legislation that attempts to normalize their lifestyle, including having pornography (especially that involving children) legalized as a valid form of expression. Rueda concluded that the homosexual community is a "reservoir of disease for the rest of society," with most of their physical and mental illnesses resulting from the continued impersonal sexual activity associated with the lifestyle. Rueda's research suggests an intensely lonely, physically and psychologically sick group of people.

In a 1993 study, the Family Research Institute (FRI) disclosed some alarming facts about the homosexual life span. They reported the median age of death in the homosexual male to be forty-two years of age, compared to a median age of seventy-five in heterosexual married men. Sadly, those who continue to choose homosexuality as a way of life choose sexual perversion over common sense and usually die without living long enough to fulfill their dreams. (Those who deny that homosexuality is a choice, please continue reading.)

The homosexual lifestyle is not propelled by any great desire to make the world a better place. As a group, that community has never delivered any significant message to humanity. The homosexual community is propelled by the selfish desires of individuals who seek sexual gratification from as many sources as possible with no thought given to the welfare of the rest of society or even to those within their own community. Proof of that fact is evident in the homosexual community's refusal to acknowledge their responsibility for perpetuating the spread of AIDS by not supporting responsible public health policy relative to the epidemic. Indeed, if homosexuals had any compassion for the members of their own community, wouldn't they do everything within their power to stop AIDS? Instead, those infected often continue their promiscuous behavior with an attitude that seems to say, "If I'm going to go, I'm going to have fun and take as many people with me as possible." Despite all of their shrieking about the failure of government to act, homosexual lobbyists have fought to stop any responsible action on the part of the government to control the spread of HIV.

Thus, it is now estimated that *87 percent* of their own community is dying from that deadly disease—a sad and disturbing revelation about the homosexual's concern for his fellow man.

It's inconceivable that a group of people would fight to keep a deadly communicable disease from being reported, but that's exactly what homosexual activists continue to do. AIDS began in the homosexual community, and it is perpetuated by the selfishness of those who refuse to stop engaging in promiscuous sex with multiple partners. These are the same people who insist that anyone who wants to stop the spread of AIDS is out to destroy their reputation by exposing their homosexual lifestyle. Long before AIDS, a confidentiality code existed that deemed it unethical for doctors to divulge a patient's medical history without permission. Though activists have yet to produce a single example of a patient's rights being violated, the homosexual lobby fights to block any legislation that would allow for random HIV testing.

Imagining that a patient's privacy was invaded, the argument is still absurd. To suggest that one person's privacy is more important than the lives of millions is ridiculous. Even so, the homosexual lobby has convinced liberal lawmakers that protecting the rest of us from AIDS is somehow less important than the "civil rights" of a minuscule minority of people who *choose* to engage in behavior they know is dangerous. As members of a nation at risk of not only infection but death, all citizens have a right to be concerned about that. (Note: There is absolutely no evidence to prove that HIV testing results in loss of privacy for a very few, but there is overwhelming evidence that failure to test is costing tens of thousands of people their lives.)

The purpose of the Center for Disease Control (CDC) is to protect the public by administering programs that help control the spread of diseases. Throughout America's history, communicable diseases like bubonic plague, typhoid, and small pox have been controlled because of the

CDC's contact-tracing efforts. Similarly, the spread of sexually transmitted diseases like syphilis and gonorrhea have been controlled because doctors treating those diseases are required by law to report the names of patients and their sexual contacts to the CDC. Once identified, the sexual partners of those infected are notified, tested, and, if necessary, treated so they don't continue to infect others. As unbelievable as it is, under pressure from homosexual activists, *the CDC has yet to categorize AIDS as a communicable disease!*

The CDC has consistently cowered under the pressure of homosexuals who fear exposure of their lifestyle and possible loss of employment if positive AIDS results are made public. For those reasons alone, the CDC has refused to make HIV testing mandatory. Undoubtedly, the spread of AIDS could have been easily controlled if the CDC had taken a responsible position from the beginning, treating AIDS as a health problem instead of the civil rights issue the homosexual lobby has made it out to be. Unfortunately for all of us, the current majority of politicians and medical experts are more concerned with political correctness than they are with telling us the truth about AIDS and then proceeding as they have proceeded with every other epidemic. The government's refusal to insist on mandatory HIV testing is more than absurd, and it puts the rest of us in grave danger of contracting AIDS and, ultimately, losing our lives.

If HIV testing were mandatory, experts believe they could identify 99.5 percent of those infected. Further, they claim the chance of a person being falsely diagnosed is almost nonexistent. As a research virologist for the United States Army, Col. Donald Burke of Walter Reed Hospital supervised the only large-scale HIV blood testing ever done. After administering literally millions of HIV blood tests, he noted only one incidence of false-positive results for every million tests given.[2]

Politicians opposed to HIV testing often cite the cost, making the implication that government would be re-

sponsible for paying for the tests. Some state governments require blood tests before marriage, and those are
always paid for by individuals; why should HIV tests be
any different? There is absolutely no logical reason why
people can't be tested for HIV at the same time that
blood is drawn for premarital tests.

Many of the politicians opposing mandatory HIV testing are the same ones who voted to spend close to $150
billion to remove asbestos from public buildings in a val-
iant effort to "protect the public health." But, according
to the *New England Journal of Medicine* (29 June 1989),
"chances are between 1 in 3 million, and 1 in 20 million
that a child may contract cancer from asbestos." (Note
the seventeen million margin; apparently, that's as close
as government "experts" could get!) By contrast, we know
for a fact that almost ten thousand people contracted
HIV from their infected marriage partners in 1990 alone.[3]
Had the interest of the majority been considered and the
HIV test added to other mandatory premarital blood tests,
perhaps many of those lives could have been saved, as
could the tens of thousands of others who subsequently
contracted the deadly disease from those victims.

Politicians are notorious for wasting taxpayer's money.
If it was determined that government should pay for HIV
testing, perhaps they could take the money from some
other "worthwhile" program—such as Project Aries, for
which politicians allocated *two million dollars* to set up a
toll-free phone line that counsels about five-hundred homosexuals to "be sexual, but be safe." Not only do homosexuals get free counseling and encouragement for their
perversion at taxpayer expense, the government pays them
twenty dollars each time they call and another five dollars
per month to call toll-free and confirm their mailing address! And, oh, in order to protect the caller's privacy,
the government is throwing in a "free" post office box.
(You'll be getting the bill for that April 15.)[4]

Homosexual activists have been consistent in labeling
researchers who are gravely concerned for the health and

welfare of all Americans homophobic. Sadly, name call-
ing almost always diverts the public's attention from the
real issue, which is how to protect all of us from the
spread of AIDS. While militant homosexuals seek to make
others appear prejudiced and full of hate, it is the mili-
tants, themselves, who have shown no concern for anyone—least of all those within their own small community.
Instead of protecting those they claim to care about, they
have only succeeded in terrorizing homosexuals into believing that HIV testing will result in their persecution. In
their hysteria, those being convinced have never made
the effort to logically think the issue through. Why would
any rational person deny a test that could save his life or
the life of his loved one? The public must be tested for
HIV, and when infection is found, doctors must be required to report the results. Contact tracing must be
done in order to control the disease, and government
must create and enforce a strict policy that punishes those
who knowingly transmit the deadly virus to others.

The entire AIDS epidemic can be traced to a single
homosexual who gave the HIV virus to at least forty
different people who, in turn, spread it to countless others. The CDC not only knew the name and whereabouts
of the carrier, they interviewed him personally on several
occasions and warned him to stop having random sex.
Knowing he was dying, the individual ignored the pleas
of the CDC and decided to have a good time before he
died and make as many people as possible suffer with
him. The CDC knew what he was doing. This all happened in the state of California, which has a law making
it a felony for anyone to knowingly spread a communicable disease, so the CDC had legal grounds to arrest
him. Still, they did nothing, allowing the infected individual to spread the disease to hundreds of people.[5] Incredibly, several years and hundreds of thousands of
patients later, the CDC's position has not changed.

As if the CDC's failure to protect the public is not
enough, government compounds the danger by promot-

ing false confidence through "Safe-sex Education." As part of their "concern" for the welfare of our children, government has taken to dispensing condoms through school-based health clinics and lying about its ability to "protect" our children from AIDS.

"Just Like Everyone Else"

In their study on the life span of homosexuals, the Family Research Institute (FRI) studied almost seven thousand death notices from homosexual newspapers and compared them to death notices from nonhomosexual newspapers. In addition to proving that the homosexual life span is shockingly low when compared to heterosexuals, research revealed much about the psychological illness in the homosexual community:

• The murder rate among homosexuals was 116 times higher than among heterosexual white males in the same age group, and 21 times higher than among blacks.

• Homosexual men experienced violent death 28 times more frequently than heterosexual white males in the same age group, and 17 times more than blacks.

• The suicide rate among homosexuals is 24 times higher than in white heterosexual males, and 30 times higher than in blacks.

• Homosexuals had a significantly higher number of heart attacks; 22 times higher than heterosexual white males, and 11 times higher than blacks.

• The median age of death is 45 for lesbians, compared to 79 for heterosexual married women.[6]

• The murder rate among lesbians was 511 times higher than that of heterosexual white females in the same age group, and the suicide rate was 705 times higher.[7]

Other studies showed that:

• Lesbian women are two to three times more likely to develop breast cancer than heterosexual women.[8]

• 9.2 percent of lesbians admit to heavy alcohol consumption, as compared to 2.4 percent of heterosexual women.[9]

• Lesbian women over the age of fifty-five smoke three times as much as other women in the same age group.[10]

Though AIDS or related illness is the number one killer of homosexuals, psychological dysfunction is an accompanying factor in most of the deaths within that community, though activists are desperate to hide that fact from the general public. Today, few people recall that homosexuality was considered a mental illness until 1973 when militant activists forced the American Psychiatric Association to remove homosexuality from their Diagnostic and Statistical Manual of Psychiatric Disorders.[11] Thus, "sexual perversion" became sexual "orientation." This begs the question, Will pedophilia and incest someday be considered "orientations," and, if so, what legal recourse will there be against child molesters?

In their efforts to have their perversity declared an "orientation," homosexual activists had considerable help from much quoted psychiatrist Dr. Richard Pillard, who proudly identifies himself as "the first openly gay psychiatrist in the United States." Pillard claims that "the psychiatrists of the future are going to be gay men who are going to infiltrate the establishment and . . . be heard." (That information will certainly make everyone eager to see a therapist!)

In an interview in the homosexual magazine *Guide*, Pillard stated his belief that "the punishment for having sex with an underage person should be a $25.00 fine." He went on to add that "people who like to have sex with minors, SM sex, or whatever, are subject to unbelievable wrath and punishment," and that (in his humble scientific opinion) "is a horrible state of affairs!" Even more frightening than the fact that Pillard gets *paid* for his opinions is the fact that he is a dean of psychiatry and full professor at Boston University![12]

Regardless of what the American Psychiatric Association says, most people still consider homosexuality a form of mental illness. Countless homosexual publications bear witness to the fact that homosexual sex is perverse, violent, and demeaning. Further, those publications show that a large number of homosexuals associate physical pain, degradation, and humiliation with sexual pleasure. Sadomasochism and prostitution are staple practices for homosexuals, indicative of the self-hatred and homophobia they often feel for themselves—certainly not an indication of a psychologically healthy group of people. While homosexuals view all dysfunction within their community as a manifestation of society's failure to accept them, research on individual homosexuals indicates that almost without exception emotional and psychological illness was a precursor to the lifestyle choice.[13]

Apart from the physical and mental diseases noted, there is overwhelming evidence that homosexuality is a sociological disease, as well. In their attempts to "normalize" their lifestyle, homosexuals are changing the traditional moral code of our country by force. The passage of prohomosexual legislation is a universal goal of the movement, and, in order for them to win the sympathy of law makers, homosexuals must be viewed as a legitimate minority by proving that they've been discriminated against. Thus, their penchant for always grouping themselves with ethnic minorities.

Of great concern to homosexuals are laws imposing any restrictions on consensual sexual practices; homosexuals want to eliminate all Age of Consent laws, including those that make sex illegal between adults and children. The implication is that children don't mind being sexually abused by adults. As unbelievable as it sounds, activists actually convinced the state of New York to legalize the use of children in pornographic films![14]

Do They Really Want Our Children?

Though they deny it, homosexuals absolutely have a preoccupation with recruiting children, and they're actively positioning themselves in places where they can influence the way our children think about their lifestyle. If such an assertion were not true, homosexuals would have no reason to be on public school campuses. Mandatory sex education curricula in many schools today fully endorses homosexuality. Recorded incidents of attempts to recruit children in public schools would fill volumes. In the interest of space, here are just a few:

ITEM: Even liberals were shocked when two lesbian teachers gave their elementary school students valentines with "900" telephone-sex numbers attached.

ITEM: The following is an excerpt from a story written by a homosexual teacher; it was published in *Blade*, a homosexual magazine:

> Then there are my favorite boys... at this point they need and seek my affection rather than that of the women teachers. They trust me, turn to me, and are more dependent on me. They even seek physical intimacy, caressing my arms or unbuttoning my shirt.... Since I feel that Gay is good, I'm a little biased in imagining that these boys might turn out to be healthily Gay identified.[15]

ITEM: In March of 1993, WNBC-TV News in New York City did a brief exposé of pedophiles in the schools. John Miller, the correspondent reporting the story, said, "We thought these guys were people who lurk around outside schools. What we found was, they lurk around *inside* the schools"[16] (emphasis added). Pedophiles always seek jobs and volunteer positions that allow them to be close to children. Certainly, not all homosexuals are pedophiles, but many pedophiles are homosexual.

In an article about the exposé, *U.S. News and World Report* revealed that in 1984 the City Board of Education in New York learned that one of the teachers featured in Miller's piece was a pedophile, yet, when the exposé aired almost ten years later, Peter Melzer was still teaching in the New York public school system.[17] Melzer boasts of his position on the steering committee of the North Ameri-

can Man/Boy Love Association (NAMBLA) and is proud
to say that he serves on the editorial board of the *NAMBLA
Bulletin,* a publication that offers advice to its readers on
how to entice children into sex. When NAMBLA members are not having sex with children, they devote themselves to the pursuits of kiddie porn and the promotion
of legislation to obliterate Age of Consent laws.
(NAMBLA's motto is "Sex after [age] eight is too late.")
It's significant to note that the International Lesbian and
Gay Association lists NAMBLA as a member even though
that group says it has no interest in recruiting children or
having sex with them. Regardless of their claims to the
contrary, the homosexual community is dependent upon
children in order for their lifestyle to survive: Homosexuals do not procreate, and that entire group faces extinction in the wake of the AIDS epidemic.

If the reader is still not convinced of the homosexual's
ambition to recruit children, consider the following declaration by Michael Swift, a radical homosexual activist.
The article appeared in the *Gay Community News* (15-21
February 1987).

> We shall sodomize your sons, emblems of your
> feeble masculinity, of your shallow dreams and
> vulgar lies. We shall seduce them in your schools,
> in your dormitories, in your gymnasiums, in your
> locker rooms, in your sports areas, in your semi-
> naries, in your youth groups, in your movie the-
> ater bathrooms . . . wherever men are with men
> together. Your sons shall become our minions and
> do our bidding. They will be recast in our image.
> They will come to crave and adore us.

Immorality 101

Perversity is being sold to our children in packages
labeled, "family life" and "marriage and family curriculum." If truth in labeling laws applied to school curricula,
they would have to be called "Immorality 101: The Pro-

motion of Promiscuity and Perversity." These courses, most of them designed to promote the acceptance of homosexuality and make promiscuity appear "normal," consume much of the time teachers used to spend teaching things like biology and nutrition. The curriculum is approved by the Sex Information and Education Council of the United States (SIECUS), which creates the guidelines for sex education classes. Since texts are approved by SIECUS, which has been (mis)represented to parents as "one of the most prestigious private educational groups in the country," most parents are under the false assumption that the material is in the best interest of children. The SIECUS guidelines reveal the mindset behind that "prestigious" group, stating that our children *must* be taught the following:

> Masturbation is physically and psychologically harmless and, alone or with a partner, it can be a "sensible alternative" to risky sexual practices.

> No form of sexual orientation or family structure is morally superior.

> Sexually active children compensate for unmet emotional needs with sex, but that usually doesn't apply to kids over fifteen.

> It is healthy to discuss erogenous zones.

> Abortion is legal, and far less risky than pregnancy.[18]

Methods

Using the SIECUS guidelines, teachers often use "role playing" to teach alternative lifestyles, forcing the government's idea of morality on America's public school children through its sex education curriculum. During role playing, students are "set up" and asked to play the parts of different characters created in the curriculum. In such "exercises," the teacher may ask a student to play the part of a young man who thinks he might be homosexual and is struggling with that possibility. The second "actor" may play the part of his best friend. One actor is (almost always) labeled "a Christian who thinks homosexuality is a sin." Another may be an openly homosexual person, male or female. One student-actor might ask, "What makes you think you're gay?" Another may ask, "How do you feel about the possibility that you might be gay?" Or, "How do you think your parents will act when they find out?" and so on. The object of the lesson is for the students to "engage in meaningful dialogue" until they each reach a conclusion about how they "feel" about homosexuality. Once each student reveals his feelings to the class (apparently, kids have no right to private feelings anymore), he must defend his position in front of his peers.

In role-playing forums, children with strong moral convictions are almost always in the minority. I have never seen, nor heard of, a role-playing set-up where actors with traditional moral values are not outnumbered at least two-to-one. Given the peer-acceptance factor, one can imagine the pressure put on that one, lone child to take a stand against the other actors in front of an entire class. Even though a child may know that certain behavior is wrong, at the age of twelve or thirteen, most place the desire for peer acceptance ahead of the desire to take a stand for what is right. Further, if not for the fact that SIECUS is forcing homosexuality on children, most would be unaware of it or, at least, indifferent. Those few who are strong enough to firmly say they think homosexuality is wrong are almost always forced to explain their "intolerance" and "insensitivity" to the rest of the class.

In his excellent book, *Shadow in the Land: Homosexuality in America*, Congressman William Dannemeyer says, "[Homosexuals] are demanding that their behavior be defended and their rights affirmed in American classrooms. In a curriculum that is supposed to be 'value free,' they want tolerance of homosexual behavior elevated to the level of a moral imperative."

The Assault on Innocence

SIECUS encourages lessons on masturbation in kindergarten and, alarmingly, the National Association for the Education of Young Children—the largest accreditation agency for preschool education in America—invited the Gay and Lesbian Caucus to make a presentation at their 1990 conference.

Comprehensive sex and AIDS education often begins in kindergarten because SIECUS has determined that tiny children should be robbed of their innocence by studying adult topics at the age of five. We must all ask why. What could possibly be the reason? Regardless of the age of your children, all parents must insist on knowing what is being taught in your schools!

The importance of schools as vehicles in transporting homosexual ideology should be obvious. The purpose of schools is to transmit ideas. (What better place to indoctrinate youth?) Homosexual activists and radical feminists have gone to great lengths to gain credibility among the gurus of secular humanism who have become the educational elites of our day. Numerous organizations devote themselves to implanting homosexual ideologies into *all* public school curricula. The Gay Teachers Association of New York City wants to "promote curriculum change in *all* subject areas to enable gay and nongay students to gain a realistic and positive concept of current gay lifestyles" (emphasis added).[19]

The National Gay Task Force, the Gay Rights National Lobby, the National Organization of Women, the Gay Academic Union, ACT UP, and Queer Nation are a few of hundreds of homosexual organizations active in schools throughout America. The Gay Task Force of the American Library Association (ALA) actively promotes homosexuality by making sure that books favorable to that lifestyle are on shelves of every public library in the country. These books are paid for with taxpayer money and can be found in most local libraries. Sadly, the books never present a realistic picture of what homosexuality really is.

Homosexual teachers in every major city in America have unified and organized in their efforts to affect pro-homosexual legislation and curriculum. The Gay Teachers Association of New York City boasts more than ten thousand members in that city alone! Members of these groups work to activate students on behalf of homosexual rights, encouraging them to organize rallies, push for prohomo-sexual clubs and curricula, and secure speakers sympathetic to their cause. Unbeknownst to most straight students and their parents, those groups are financed with student activity funds.

Given that the homosexual lifestyle involves same-gender sex, sadomasochism, homosexual prostitution, child/adult sex, and other well-documented perversions too disgusting to mention here, we can assume that the homosexual movement is out to censor *all* curricula until it promotes acceptance of those practices as "normal." The homosexual community is demanding that the rest of society develop "a realistic and positive concept" about sexual perversion. Anyone with a stomach strong enough to read homosexual publications or look at some of the sex education texts currently being used in our public schools would certainly question the value of such a demand. Indeed, is it even possible for a rational thinker to think positively about a behavior so obviously destructive to everyone?

Minority Rules

Alfred Kinsey was a much-quoted authority on the subject of the sexual habits of the American people until he was exposed as a fraud by his peers. It is from Kinsey's report on sexual behavior that the homosexual lobby quotes that "10% of the population is gay." For several years, there has been overwhelming evidence that Kinsey's statistic is way too high and terribly flawed.

Kinsey used fifty-three hundred men as subjects for his study—25 percent of whom were prisoners known to engage in homosexual behavior; that is hardly a cross section of the American people. Further, a large number of those prisoners were *sex offenders*, many of whom had been recruited into the survey from sex lectures where they had gone for counseling. Two hundred of the men in Kinsey's "random test group"—almost 4 percent—were male prostitutes! Kinsey had only a few subjects who admitted to ever attending church, and other groups were not represented at all. Given the fact that as many as 50 percent of those asked will refuse to participate in sex surveys, it should be obvious that the sexually unconventional are more prone to discuss the intimate details of their lives than are other people.[20]

While not admitting that they've been intentionally misleading the public, both *Time* and *Newsweek* recently said they unwittingly helped to advance the homosexual movement by presenting the one-in-ten figure as fact and ignoring the counsel of those who said the figure was exaggerated. *Newsweek* said, "Evidence suggests that ideology, not sound science, has perpetuated a 1-in-10 myth."[21]

The U.S. Census Report

In contrast to the Kinsey Report, surveys far more comprehensive have been taken, indicating that though 6 percent of the population admits to a homosexual experience (usually during adolescence when youth experiments with all sorts of things), *less than 1 percent* of those surveyed expressed an exclusive preference for homosexuality.[22] Continuing surveys done by the U.S. Census Bureau (for the Centers for Disease Control) confirm those statistics. The Census Bureau polls about fifty thousand people annually, compared to the fifty-three hundred that Kinsey surveyed once almost fifty years ago. Their data suggests that even incidental homosexual behavior occurs in less than 2 percent of men, and the incidence of homosexuality in women averages about half that. In their report, published in 1993, the U.S. Census Bureau determined that only 1.5 percent of the population claims to be homosexual or lesbian—nowhere near the 10 percent that homosexual activists continue to claim in spite of the facts.

An accurate account of the minuscule number of homosexuals in America is important because it serves to emphasize the power of their movement within the political arena. Quite clearly, less than 2 percent of the population is threatening to seize control of state and federal governments in the areas of public health and education. Significantly, the number of people opposing the homosexual lifestyle outnumbers those supporting it by about twenty-eight to one, but homosexuals are far better organized and much louder. The strength and determination of the homosexual lobby cannot be underestimated. If progress is going to be made to combat the spread of homosexual ideology, those who oppose that lifestyle must be as well organized and as politically active as the radical homosexual activists who are forcing prohomosexual legislation and curriculum on the rest of us!

The banshee-like wails of the angry homosexuals heard outside the Hamilton Square Church, as described in the first chapter of this book, presage the death of a generation of children who are falling victim to the lies of the homosexual community—lies spreading as quickly, and proving as deadly, as the AIDS virus. Homosexuals are infiltrating our schools and attempting to seize control of the minds of our children. With the help of the National Education Association and SIECUS, our children are being subtly desensitized and taught that sexual perversion is absolutely normal.

Homosexual Curriculum

As reported in the May/June (1994) issue of *Education Newsline*, a history teacher at Homestead High School in Cupertino, California, recently gave his class a position paper titled, "Heterosexuality: Can it Be Cured?" (When confronted, the teacher was, understandably, at a loss to explain what his paper had to do with history.) With subtitles like "Heterosexuality, Medical Hazard"; "Mental and Psychological Hazard"; and "Treatment and Cures," the paper used totally distorted statistics to persuade teens of the alleged horrendous psychological and social hazards of life as a *non*homosexual! The paper concludes with the following statement: "Lastly, we suggest widespread and total sterilization of the heterosexual population." (This would soon be a lonely planet given the fact that homosexuals do not reproduce.) Parents in Cupertino are taking steps to have the teacher fired.

The doctrine of homosexuality is invading every aspect of education, and seldom is it subtle. Elementary school curricula like the controversial "Children of the Rainbow" and disturbingly bold programs like Project 10 are invading campuses all across America, usually by way of intimidation as small groups of homosexual activists intrude on local school board meetings, violently demanding that parents submit to teaching sexual perversion to children. Sadly, many of them do.

Project 10 is one of many prohomosexual, school-sponsored programs paid for with taxpayers' money. Project 10 is a course that offers "emotional support, information, resources and referral to young people who identify themselves as lesbian, gay or bisexual." The course is mandatory in the state of California, where children are forced to listen to homosexuals like teacher Virginia Uribe "share" about the different ways she has sex—as if that's something our children need to know! During Project 10 indoctrinations, teachers like Uribe are paid with tax dollars to tell children that attraction to members of the same sex is "normal" and that homosexuality should be accepted as a "viable alternative lifestyle." Reportedly, one lecturer gleefully told his class, "at least 10% of you are gay—some of you just don't know it!" His presentation caused one young woman to remark that "if a kid doesn't think he's gay when he goes in there, he's convinced he is when he comes out!" Following the lecture, speakers answer questions, and no subject is taboo.

While homosexuality is being presented in schools and in the media as the newest fad, the *Washington Post* reported a significant increase in the number of teens questioning their sexuality (July 1993). Impressionable children are being force-fed a doctrine which states that the politically correct thing to do is to accept the homosexual lifestyle. Given their need for peer acceptance, it is likely that children will be outwardly accepting of homosexuality because they think their friends accept it; inwardly, they may reject the idea completely. Also, the consideration must be made that teens are rebellious by nature and may view the acceptance of homosexuality—or even the announcement of a homosexual preference—as a sure way to upset their parents. Still another consideration is that some adolescents actually *are* genuinely questioning their sexuality. Since children are being taught that perversion is normal, it's highly possible that some may consider themselves abnormal because they're *not* aroused by perversion! Certainly, questions about sexuality are a normal part of adolescent development, but that does not mean that children should be coached into homosexual sex!

At taxpayer expense, the Office of Counseling and Guidance Services for the Los Angeles Unified School District prepared a pamphlet for use in Project 10. In that pamphlet (made available to any child in California public schools), a sixteen-year-old girl gave an intimate account of a lesbian encounter she had at the age of twelve with her female teacher. In case any child reading the pamphlet does not understand what oral sex is, the girl explains it in explicit detail.[23] Given the age of the child, we can assume that the teacher instigated the encounter. Aside from the fact that programs like Project 10 absorb class time which could be *much* better spent, what gives government the right to teach perversion in public schools and force immorality upon our children?

In most cases, public school programs not accompanied by requests for additional funds are not voted on, so curriculum like Project 10 is almost always implemented without the knowledge, consent, or approval of the parents who are unwittingly forced to pay for it. Almost assuredly, if your child attends public school, he is being indoctrinated into accepting homosexuality and other perversions as natural. While school districts claim that sex education classes are designed to "stress sensitivity, tolerance and acknowledgment of alternative lifestyles without endorsing a sexual orientation," that simply is *not* true. In itself, the curriculum is an unqualified endorsement of sexual perversion. Twenty years ago, the pamphlet just mentioned would have been banned from use—an indication of how deeply mired in filth this country has become following the formation of SIECUS, the intrusion of Planned Parenthood into the classroom, and the surge of homosexual activism.

The literature used in classrooms today—which the NEA claims "does not endorse any particular sexual orientation"—is sexually explicit, condones promiscuity, and paints a rosy, completely erroneous and biased picture of homosexual life. We have yet to see any prohomosexual curriculum which truthfully addresses the very serious issue of the disproportionate physical and mental health problems present in that community.

Several years ago, the Department of Health, Education and Welfare commissioned a massive evaluation of sex education classes in public schools, hiring an independent agency (Mantech, Inc.) to conduct the survey. In its final statement, Mantech reported that full acceptance of homosexuality and masturbation is the projected outcome of a substantial number of sex education classes. Researchers found that children who participated in the classes were, indeed, more accepting of homosexuality and other perversions.[24] Given the impressionable character of young people, the results of the survey shouldn't surprise us. Remember, the survey was not done by any "radical-right-wing-Christian-activist" group. It was done by the U.S. Department of Health, Education and Welfare!

In Your Own Back Yard

If you think homosexuals are not working hard to promote their agenda in your state, think again:

MASSACHUSETTS: Governor Weld claims a need to "create an atmosphere of dignity and respect for gay youth" in Massachusetts schools. Weld thinks schools should adopt antidiscrimination policies (desensitization curriculum) and form support groups for homosexual students.[25] It's hard to say just when politicians became so preoccupied with sexual behavior, but, at some point, they assumed the duty of legislating immorality.

WISCONSIN: Included with courses in "Animal Sciences," "Wetlands and Wildlife," and "Careers in Agriculture," the State 4-H Congress offered a seminar called "What's It Like To Be Different," in which they instructed the Future Farmers of America in the fine art of "sexual orientations that set people apart."[26] No one at 4-H cared to speculate as to what the course has to do with farming.

NEBRASKA: According to a study guide produced for the school district, counselors should not use the word "marriage" when communicating with students. The Omaha School District wants to avoid any appearance of "heterosexism," which they think may promote the idea that heterosexuality is superior to homosexuality.[27]

MINNESOTA: In the interest of promoting the homo-sexual agenda in Minnesota's schools, the Education Exploration Center in Minneapolis made the following plea to readers of a homosexual magazine:

> The Education Exploration Center is soliciting articles for a curriculum-anthology on teaching gay and lesbian issues in secondary and elementary schools. We want articles from teachers, students and parents—articles on experiences like being the only lesbian in the local PTA, *how to slip gay and lesbian issues into lesson plans*, student reactions to a gay speaker . . . how to organize a lesbian and gay teachers association. (emphasis added)[28]

Given the space, further examples could be given for every state in the union.

Not only do many school boards sanction homosexuality, they actually seek ways to promote it. The now infamous "Children of the Rainbow" curriculum encourages teachers to discuss homosexuality, saying that "if teachers do not discuss lesbian and gay issues, they are not likely to come up." (As the kids say, "No, *duh!*") The curriculum asserts that children "need actual experiences via creative play, books, visitors, etc., in order for them to view lesbians and gays as real people to be respected and appreciated." Imagine, for a moment, the implications of "creative play" if your child happens to have a homosexual teacher like the twelve-year-old mentioned previously.

A Proper Response

Those who share God's view that homosexuality is a sinful, unnatural perversion are always quoted out of context and tagged "homophobic" when what they actually are, is *righteously angry*. God is adamant in His disapproval of homosexuality; He says clearly that homosexual relationships are unnatural and wrong. God calls homosexuality a "perversion"[29] and says that homosexuals will not enter the Kingdom of God.[30] Those who believe in the God of the Bible must form their opinions about the issue based on that Truth.

Homosexuality is a grievous sin that destroys lives. Nevertheless, God's will is for Christians to show Christ's love and compassion to *all* people whether or not they agree with the lifestyle those people are living. Given that all believers are promised the "mind of Christ," it is quite possible for Christians to love sinners while still hating their sin. The hatred of homosexual men and women is a sin as vile to God as the act of homosexuality itself. Therefore, our challenge is to view the issue of homosexuality with the tolerance and understanding of a Divine God who forgives everything and has unlimited perspective. The goal is not to pass judgment, but to relay facts, minus the euphemistic generalizations and political double-speak of liberal media.

"Christians" who reinterpret the Word of God in a pursuit to justify sin cannot change the Truth about what the Bible says. This applies to those who call themselves "Christian" but hate homosexuals, and it applies to homosexuals who call themselves Christians. Homosexuals must understand that one cannot be both a chronic sinner and a child of God. Scripture says, "No one who is born of God will continue to sin."[31] By way of definition, a Christian is one who follows Jesus and seeks to live his or her life in obedience to God. That means that one strives to avoid all sin, including the sexual sins of adultery, homosexuality, bestiality, and incest.

Those who don't consider the Bible at all must still look rationally at the issue of homosexuality, disregarding the deceptive issue of political correctness. Regardless of one's relationship to God or His view regarding morality, we are all forced to live in a world infested with the reality of AIDS.

Sticks and Stones

While homosexual activists want the world to believe that anyone who disagrees with their choices hates them, that simply is not true. Homosexuals always tag those who oppose them as homophobes because name-calling turns the focus from their sin, and it points a finger of accusation at the person delivering the facts. Further, name-calling casts a shadow of doubt on one's credibility and turns the attention from what's being said to an examination of the person who's saying it. That strategy always confuses the listener which is exactly what the name-caller wants. Any time there's name-calling during debate, you can be assured that the one doing the name-calling is losing the argument.

The public deserves to know the facts about the homosexual agenda, and this author has dug deeply to get them; but that does not mean that I hate homosexuals. Indeed, I want to know the truth about public education, but that doesn't mean that I hate teachers. Because America (at least for now) is still a free country, we all deserve to know the truth about government, but that doesn't mean that we hate politicians. As with obstinate children, homosexual activists turn to name-calling when their actions can be justified in no other way than to simply point a finger at someone else. Though I do not hate homosexuals, I am deeply concerned over the choices they make because those choices directly affect me, my family, and the society in which we live. Further, I believe the consequences of homosexual behavior are detrimental to an entire nation of people—the majority of whom do not agree that the lifestyle is at all "acceptable." I am angry that politicians allow such a small minority of people to intimidate them into creating laws and public health policies that place an entire nation morally and physically at risk. As one whose tax dollars are being spent to advance the homosexual agenda, I believe I have a right to be angry when less than 2 percent of the population can force their lifestyle on the other 98 percent who may or may not agree with them.

Biology or Beguilement?

The success of the homosexual agenda depends upon keeping the public confused and ignorant about the facts. Homosexuals want us to believe that they are "born that way" when there is absolutely no scientific evidence to bear that out. Even a special task force appointed to study the issue for the National Institute of Mental Health, concluded that a "psychosexual object *choice* is the only obvious difference between homosexuals and heterosexuals" (emphasis added).[32] There you have it. *Object choice.* Still, when the liberal media refers to the "latest scientific study" suggesting that homosexuality is biologically based, they are seldom (if ever) pressed to produce any facts.

A study frequently quoted as producing proof that homosexuality is genetically induced was conducted in 1991 by neurobiologist Simon LeVay at the Salk Institute for Biological Studies in La Jolla, California.

In his study, LeVay analyzed brain tissue from forty-one cadavers and found that one group of neurons in the hypothalamus was almost three times larger in heterosexual men than it was in homosexual men or heterosexual women. Specifically, LeVay studied four separate groupings of cells located at the front of the hypothalamus, the small region of the brain known to the medical community as INAH—the interstitial nuclei of the anterior hypothalamus. INAH is the section of the brain known to help regulate male sexual behavior.

Even though many technical aspects of LeVay's study were questioned within the scientific community, the liberal media and homosexual activists grabbed the story and continue to hurl LeVay's conclusions like a pie in the face of anyone who dares to suggest that homosexuality is a *chosen* lifestyle. Newspapers and magazines headlined the study, suggesting proof of "a structural difference

between the brains of homosexual and heterosexual men."
News reporters on every network across the country presented LeVay's hypothesis as fact, praising his findings as
confirmation that homosexuals are "born that way."
LeVay's study immediately became the subject of several
television talk shows, offering homosexual men and
women a forum through which to tell audiences that
from early childhood they "knew they were homosexual"
and that they "couldn't help being gay."

What the media didn't mention was that nineteen of
LeVay's forty-one cadavers were homosexual men. Further, all nineteen of those homosexuals had died of AIDS,
as had six of the heterosexual men and one of the six
women.[33] It was never mentioned that well over half of
LeVay's subjects died of AIDS—a disease which is known
to affect the brain. In addition, the areas of the brain
LeVay studied are smaller than snowflakes, and neurosci-
entists do not even agree on the proper way to measure
the region. Some think the most accurate gauge is the
volume; others believe it's the number of neurons.[34] Because AIDS adversely affects the brain, and 87 percent of
homosexuals are currently dying of AIDS,[35] it is impossible to conclude whether the difference in the brain
tissue is the cause or effect of the behavior.

The media also failed to mention that LeVay is a
homosexual, a fact that may have slanted his perception
regarding the results of his study. As with all forms of sin,
man strives to find a way to blame someone or something
else in order to make himself less accountable for his
actions. To prove that one "can't help it" is to absolve
man of his responsibility to control himself. In addition,
"proof" of a genetic cause can do much to help homosexuals in arguing for their political agenda. If activists
can convince the public that homosexuals are "born that
way" and are no more responsible for their behavior than
a black man is responsible for the color of his skin or a
dwarf responsible for his size, they will gain sympathy
from the public and ground for political advancement.

Activists know that if the public comes to view homosexuals in the same way they view ethnic minorities and handicapped people, the door will swing wide open for them to enter the political arena with an agenda that is repulsive to most of the people who will be supporting it with their hard-earned tax dollars.

Another recent study that falsely reported "proof that gays are born that way" was done by Dr. Dean Hamer at the National Cancer Institute. At this writing, no one has determined how Dr. Hamer was able to divert much-needed dollars intended for *cancer* research into a study of sexual orientation. Nor does anyone know what it's costing in dollars or lives as cancer patients wait for a cure. The research continues for a third consecutive year, and, according to a coauthor of the study, Hamer's research requires full use of the lab and leaves little time for anything else.

Wanting to give Hamer the benefit of the doubt, the Family Research Institute (FRI) inquired as to possible research in the area of Kaposi's Sarcoma, a form of cancer linked to AIDS. Dr. Stella Hu, an associate in the study, told FRI that no tests for Kaposi's Sarcoma had been run in any of the subjects because research was limited to the study of sexual orientation.[36]

In his study, Hamer sought to prove a link between DNA markers on the X chromosome and homosexuality; his report suggests that homosexuality is transmitted to the child by the mother through the X chromosome. In order to secure subjects for his study, Hamer placed an ad in a homosexual publication and found forty pairs of homosexual brothers who agreed to participate. Once all subjects were examined, Hamer determined that thirty-three of the forty pairs of brothers shared identical genetic markers in a particular region of the X chromosome. This led to his conclusion that homosexuality is genetically influenced. Hamer went on to report a "99% [chance] that at least one subtype of male sexual orientation is genetically influenced."[37]

As noted by Dr. Paul Cameron, Hamer's study contains many scientific limitations that were ignored by the media. First, "a correlation for specific genetic markers does not imply that a gene ... caused the brothers' homosexuality," Cameron noted. "Results could [point to other] traits shared by these subjects and disproportionately common in gays."[38] For example, both could be left-handed or colorblind.

Further, seven of the forty pairs of brothers did not share any of the markers—a fact that led several researchers to conclude that homosexuality was *not* the result of genetic influence. Also, closer examination posed questions about the thirty-three pairs of brothers who *did* share identical markers: A mother can be either heterozygous, which means that her first X chromosome is genetically different from the others, or homozygous, which means that each child would receive the same marker, regardless of his sexual orientation. Hamer based his conclusions on the assumption that each mother was heterozygous even though he didn't test twenty-two of the mothers of the thirty-three concordant pairs of brothers! Further, Hamer didn't check the same genetic markers in the heterosexual brothers of his subjects; had he found them to have the same markers, his report would be completely baseless. From a scientific perspective, Hamer conducted a study with *no control group*. Additionally, all genes influence several different physical and behavioral characteristics, so the probability that a single gene would significantly affect behavior as complicated as homosexuality is highly improbable.

Nowhere in Hamer's study does he address the issue of homosexuals who leave that lifestyle and never again engage in homosexual behavior. Nor does he mention the "straight" men who decide to participate in homosexual activity. If Hamer had successfully proven that people were "born that way," he'd have to explain the phenomena of those two groups of people.

Like LeVay, Hamer is a homosexual, though *Science* magazine didn't think it necessary to mention *that* when it published his report. Nor did they mention that several of the doctors cited in Hamer's literature reviews as authorities who supported his findings were also homosexual. Objective observers will ask what the motivation for Hamer's study was (Homosexual politics? Acceptance of the homosexual lifestyle? Self-justification in order to defend his own lifestyle choice?). If Hamer had no hidden motives, why didn't he divulge the fact that he is homosexual when he released the results of his study?

Hamer's report refers to homosexuality as a "naturally occurring variation," and that's how he wants society to view it. If a person "can't help it," "it" is somehow more acceptable. When "it" becomes acceptable, "it" can be legislated, and the homosexual agenda can move forward. In fact, the theory of genetic homosexuality has been generally discarded, today; no serious scientists suggest that a simple cause-effect relationship applies.[39]

What You Can Do

Tragically, kids today are learning a preoccupation with sex and sexual perversion through the liberal media and the public school classroom. Athletes and entertainers with AIDS are heralded as heroes and eulogized as saints when they have the morals of alley cats. It is the responsibility of parents to discuss societal values with their children and to impress upon them the fact that no amount of money, talent, or public adoration can compensate for a lack of morality. It's important for children to know that while people get by with a lot in this life, sin has eternal consequences. No liberal media, no school curriculum, no homosexual activist, or representative from Planned Parenthood can alter that fact. What matters is what God says, not what man says.

Parents cannot stop homosexuality or sexual promiscuity, but we can do much to influence public school curriculum and government policy. If we become as well-organized and loud as the feminist and homosexual lobbies, and as aggressive and demanding as they are when it comes to involvement in public education and politics, we can set America on a course toward a return to traditional morality. Some suggestions follow:

1. We must besiege local politicians with demands for responsible public health policy and mandatory HIV testing.

2. We must let individual school boards know that we do not accept the premise of homosexuality as normal, and we do not want that ideology taught to our children. Those opposed to homosexuality must demand the removal of all prohomosexual curricula and special projects. At the very least, parents have a right to "opt" their children out of courses and lectures they view as immoral.

3. We must learn the names of our school board members and find out where they stand on issues important to us; we must make our presence known at school board meetings. Beginning on the local level, we must scrutinize school boards to identify those who are forcing filth on our children through public school curricula. Once identified, we must organize to force them from office. As a taxpayer, you have a right to attend school board meetings.

4. We must go to our local public libraries and request a list of prohomosexual books for children, examine those books, and make sure that other taxpayers know what their dollars are buying.

5. We must expose Kinsey's one-in-ten lie; if someone quotes the figure or if you see it written in your local newspaper, deliver the facts as quoted in the *Wall Street Journal*, 31 March 1993. Remembering that the "2.5% majority" is far more vocal and abusive than the rest of society, parents must be organized and prepared to stand their ground.

6. Parents have a right to know what their children are being taught, but the school district will not offer the information; you must ask for it. Request to see teachers' manuals, textbooks, and accompanying curricula for classes. If you're refused, demand to see it; you have the right. If they still refuse, see an attorney.

7. Expect confrontation and militant action from homosexual groups; it's inevitable.

8. Encourage your church to become active in community politics.

9. Speak up! Write letters! Call your school board members and political representatives! Tell the truth! If you know a company endorses homosexual activism, through sponsorship of "gay games," parades, etc., alert your church and write letters. If you know a company openly refuses to sponsor such activities, write and tell them you support them and will buy their products.

Government was never designed to force itself into the private lives of individual families, and it has no business doing so. Once government impinges the rights of the people, change can only take place when the people stand against government intrusion and act on their own behalf. Public schools must be warned to abandon their efforts to force immorality on our children, and parents must demand that teachers concentrate on teaching literacy skills.

If you're a teacher committed to traditional moral principles, you can have a profound effect on the children you teach by refusing to administer lessons that you know violate God's law.

We cannot be discouraged. All over America, concerned citizens are taking action against school boards that are forcing the radical homosexual agenda upon innocent children. Recently, the state of Colorado steadfastly supported Amendment 2, which rejected the idea of special rights for homosexuals. Enraged with their defeat, militant homosexuals called for tourists to "boycott" the state. In spite of their frenzied efforts, the Colorado tourism industry reported a record-breaking year.

Profamily activists in Philadelphia were successful in forcing politicians to refuse passage of a domestic partnership law for homosexuals.

In the state of Wisconsin, parents organized to pressure Milwaukee's public schools to drop plans to establish special services for homosexual students.

Voters in Cincinnati overwhelmingly passed a measure prohibiting special protections for homosexuals. Though homosexual activists got a temporary restraining order, at this writing, the citizens of Cincinnati are steadfastly standing their ground.

Instead of being discouraged by the success of the homosexual movement, we should be greatly encouraged; they've proven that a minute segment of society can rule the majority. That knowledge should inspire all of us. If 2.5 percent of the population can lead a nation toward moral destruction, certainly the other 97.5 percent can restore a nation to greatness.

Endnotes

1. Enrique T. Rueda, *The Homosexual Network: Private Lives and Public Policy* (Old Greenwich, Conn.: The Devin Adair Company, 1982), 49.

2. Stanley Monteith, M.D., *AIDS: The Unnecessary Epidemic* (Sevierville, Tenn: Covenant House Books, 1992), 78-80.

3. Ibid., 50.

4. James P. Snelling, "Federal Government Spends $2 Million for Homosexual Hotline," *The New York Guardian* (September 1992).

5. Monteith, *AIDS*, 61-66.

6. Paul Cameron, Ph.D., et al, "The Homosexual Lifespan" (Family Research Institute, Inc.), 9.

7. Ibid., 3.

8. *Cancer Weekly* (15 February 1993).

9. Ibid.

10. Ibid.

11. Ronald Bayer, *Homosexuality And American Psychiatry, The Politics of Diagnosis* (New York: Basic Books, Inc., 1981), 77.

12. *Guide*, "Gay Travel, Entertainment, Politics, & Sex" (February 1992), as cited in *The Family Research Report* (September-October 1993).

13. Rueda, *Homosexual Network*.

14. "Court Strikes Down Law Preventing 'Kiddie Pornography,'" *Courier Journal*, Rochester, N.Y. (20 May 1981).

15. Bill Springman, "What a Gay Male Teacher Offers Children," *Blade* (20 March 1981).

16. John Leo, "Pedophiles in the Schools," *U.S. News and World Report* (11 October 1993): 37.

17. Ibid.

18. George Grant and Mark A. Horne, *Legislating Immorality* (Chicago; Franklin, Tenn.: Legacy Communications, Moody Press, 1993), 76.

19. Promotional brochure on file, Gay Teachers Association of New York City.

20. J. Gordon Muir, "Homosexuals and the 10% Fallacy," *The Wall Street Journal* (31 March 1993).

21. Patrick Rogers "How Many Gays Are There?" *Newsweek* (15 February 1993): 46.

22. Muir, "Homosexuals."

23. Pamphlet on file with author.

24. Douglas Kirby et al., Public Health Service, "An Analysis of U.S. Sex Education Programs and Evaluation Methods,"

U.S. Department of Health, Education and Welfare (Report No. CDC-2021-79-DK-FR).

25. *The New York Times* (4 July 1993).

26. Brochure on file with author.

27. *World Herald* (30 September 1993).

28. "Gay and Lesbian Curriculum Anthology," *Gay Insurgent*, 1980, no. 6, 62.

29. Romans 1:26-27.

30. 1 Corinthians 6:9-10.

31. 1 John 3:9.

32. E. Hooker, "National Institute of Mental Health Task Force on Homosexuality: Final Report and Background Papers," as cited on p. 3 of the FRI's report on the homosexual life span.

33. Christine Gorman, "Are Gay Men Born That Way?" *Time* (9 September 1991): 60.

34. Sharon Begley with David Gelman, "What Causes People to Be Homosexual?" *Newsweek* (9 September 1991): 52.

35. Cameron, et. al., "Homosexual Lifespan," 5.

36. Dr. Paul Cameron, "National Cancer Institute Scandal: Gay Rights Instead of Cancer Research," *Family Research Report* (September-October 1993): 1, 6.

37. D.H. Hamer, et al, "A Linkage between DNA Markers on the X Chromosome and Male Sexual Orientation," reported in *Science*, Robert Pool, "Evidence for Homosexuality Gene," (16 July 1993): 291–292.

38. Ibid.

39. Congressman William Dannemeyer, *Shadow In the Land: Homosexuality in America* (San Francisco, Calif.: Ignatius Press, 1989), 9, quoting William H. Masters, Virginia E. Brown, and Robert C. Kolodny, from *Human Sexuality* (Boston: Ignatius, 1984), 319.

5

Sex-ed Curriculum:
Schooled in Immorality

To the pure, all things are pure, but to those who are corrupted and do not believe, nothing is pure. In fact, both their minds and consciences are corrupted. They claim to know God, but by their actions they deny him. They are detestable, disobedient and unfit for doing anything good.

—Titus 1:15-16

Premarital intercourse does have its definite values as a training ground for marriage or some other committed relationship. . . . In this sense, boys and girls who start having intercourse when they're adolescents . . . will find that it's a big help. . . . It's like taking a car out on a test run before you buy it.

—From the eighth-grade sex-ed text, *Boys and Sex.*

Four-fifths of our states either require or encourage the teaching of sex education. "Sex-ed" can mean legitimate instruction in simple biological reproductive facts, or it can mean the promotion of promiscuity and the demonstration of how to use contraceptive devices. In many cities in America, sex-ed programs focus on the *act* of sex and contraceptive information and distribution. Courses labeled "comprehensive" *must* include information about contraceptives and abortions and where to get them. In those courses, children are told everything conceivable about the physical aspect of sexual intercourse, but they are given no guidance regarding its moral and emotional implications because the Sex Information and Education Council of the United States (SIECUS) dictates that curriculum must be "values-neutral." The challenge to parents is to know what kind of sex-ed curricula their school district is using. Parents must ask for the curriculum and study it carefully, paying close attention to the focus, presentation, and content of the information. Alarmingly, even the most responsible parents are often oblivious to the impact that sex-ed is having on their children.

For the most part, it never occurs to parents that they need to protect their children from the same public school system that was trusted by their parents before them. It is unbelievable to think that children are being exposed to pornography in our public schools, but, in many districts across America, that is exactly what's happening. *The New Our Bodies, Ourselves* sex-ed text features sections on "defining orgasm" and "learning to masturbate." In another text, *Learning About Sex*, author Gary Kelly tells teens that sadomasochism and bondage "may be very acceptable and safe." He further alleges that "a fair percentage of people probably have some sort of sexual contact with an animal during their lifetimes" and that there "are no indications that such animal contacts are harmful."[1] Almost as shocking as the content of Kelly's book is the fact that it was placed on the "Best Books for Young Adults List" by the American Library Association!

In the state of Washington, high school students receive "safe sex" kits at the beginning of each school year. The kits include condoms, lubricants, and something called "dental dams"—prophylactic devices designed to promote "safe" oral-anal homosexual stimulation. Kits include instructions on the use of each item. Students can get as many kits as they want at no cost to them because those kits are paid for with your tax dollars.[2] It's quite possible that the large majority of parents in Washington State are unaware of the kits. What parent would think to ask his child, "Did you get your dental dams today?" The difficult reality is that many parents simply do not communicate with their children.

The liberal dogma preaches that "we live in a different world today, and parents just have to accept that." Sadly, many have. And, in accepting that philosophy without resistance, parents have unwittingly given the destiny of their children over to godless humanists and, in the process, have all but rendered themselves useless to implement change. It's time for parents to assert themselves on behalf of the welfare of their children and to demand that public education *cease* its sexual assault on the minds of America's youth. Parents must realize that there is power in numbers, and we actually can—and must—do something to reverse the tide. Those who have failed to take a firm stand for morality must do so now. Parents in Washington State who are angered by the presumptions of those who are giving safe-sex kits to their children must demand that the practice be stopped immediately. They must find out who is responsible for implementing the program and take appropriate action as determined by the majority.

Washington State is merely one example; children in every state in America are being victimized by a minority of activists determined to destroy the moral fiber of our youth. The way to keep your district from being victimized is to know for certain what your children are being taught. The best way to get information is to ask your children. The subject of what they're learning in school should be brought up frequently and, certainly, not limited just to the subject of sex education. In addition, parents must speak with teachers and administrators in an effort to learn where they stand on the issues that affect children's moral determinations. Parents have a right to view textbooks and curricula and to study teachers' manuals and methods in all subjects.

Parents often disregard warnings about sex-ed courses, certain that their school district isn't using offensive curricula. Sex-ed is usually not dinner-table conversation; oftentimes, parents just don't think to discuss it. Many children would never bring it up because they're simply too embarrassed to discuss what they're learning. Most are not as embarrassed by the topics as they are embarrassed by the way those topics are presented. Much of the curriculum is designed to strip children of their modesty and to make those who are chaste feel abnormal. The goal of much sex-ed curricula is to make children question the morality of church and parents and to desensitize them to promiscuity and perversion until they come to view those sins as normal. As never before, parents must superintend education. The gravest mistake we can make is to assume that "it isn't happening here."

Based on the assumption that children will be more responsible if they just have more information, many sex-ed courses have succeeded in telling kids of *all* ages far more than they ought or need to know. Responsible educators must stop and question the value of discussing intimate sexual conduct and deviances with children and teaching masturbation in elementary school classrooms. Moreover, they must question the *methods* used in teaching sex-ed topics. What value is there in having a classroom full of innocent children design and discuss a list of profane slang words for intimate body parts? How will knowing the details of homosexual sex and other perversities encourage children to become better adults? Will knowing the proper way to put on a condom strengthen a child's mind or challenge him intellectually? Have we forgotten that *literacy* is the only mandate of public education?

Discussions of sexual acts and perversities with very young children can cause them to become troubled and confused as a result of learning too much too soon. Further, thoughts of perversions like child molestation, sado-masochism, and incest can be frightening to small children. A generation of youth preoccupied with sex is the dubious legacy that SIECUS and the NEA are leaving this nation. The same children who are preoccupied with sex in elementary school grow up to be preoccupied with it in junior high and high school and, often, adulthood. That fact is substantiated by the continually increasing rate of sexual promiscuity, teen pregnancies, sexually transmitted diseases, and violent sexual crimes in this country.

The absurd idea that children as young as *five-years-old* must be exposed to the intimate details of sexual intercourse is even raising eyebrows in the psychiatric community, as doctors fear children may become fixed on the need for exhibitionistic and voyeuristic pleasure later in life. Dr. Melvin Anchell notes a "vast amount of psychoanalytic experience suggests that the majority of adult perverts are products of premature sexual seduction in early childhood." He asserts that "a child can be seduced . . . by overexposure to sexual activities, *including sex courses in the classroom*" (emphasis added).[3] Children as young as three years of age are being exposed to sex instruction that demonstrates nudity, genital anatomy, and shows how humans and animals mate. Sex education, as endorsed and approved by SIECUS and presented in large part by Planned Parenthood (through their own curricula, guest speakers, etc.), is dangerously designed to entice children into having sex before they're psychologically ready.

Between the ages of six and twelve, children experience a latent period when direct sexual feelings lie dormant. During that time, sexual energy is redirected by the mind and used in other ways. According to Sigmund Freud, much of a child's moral development takes place

during latency, and powerful components for every cultural purpose are acquired during that time. Studies show
that, largely because of sexual latency, children between
the ages of six and twelve are the most educable. Not
surprisingly, Planned Parenthood aims much of its sex-ed
curriculum at that age group, *knowing* that doing so is
harmful to children because it interferes with proper sexual
maturation by keeping sexual impulses stirred up during
the latent period.[4] It is no coincidence that for the first
time in history psychopathy in preteen children is increasing at an alarming rate. (Consider the recent inci-
dent of two ten-year-old boys who bludgeoned a two-year-
old to death in London.) Nor is it a coincidence that the
number of adolescents admitted to hospitals for depres-
sion has tripled, while adolescent suicide has increased by
200 percent in the past twenty years.[5]

SIECUS, aided by Planned Parenthood, is the ultimate child rapist, hiding on school campuses all across
America. By the time they "finish" with some children,
the psychological damage is so pervasive that it affects
them for the rest of their lives. Young girls who have
been made to feel that modesty and purity are unaccept-
able will give in to young boys preoccupied with proving
their manhood. When both are left feeling dirty and
deceived by the lie, they will move on to another partner
hoping to find there the "sexual fulfillment" they've been
taught exists. The things of childhood will be set aside to
make way for the selfish, immediate gratification they've
been taught they have a "right" to. If a pregnancy should
result from one of those meaningless unions, Planned
Parenthood will be there to "guide" your daughter to the
nearest abortuary; if it's "only an STD [sexually transmitted disease]," they will have a "free clinic" near your
home—maybe even on the school campus. If AIDS is the
result of the early sexual activity encouraged by morals-
neutral curriculum, you're on your own.

Do We Really Need Sex-ed?

Planned Parenthood wants everyone to believe that all children are going to be sexually active, and, thus, sex-ed is needed to teach them how to be "sexually safe." But, according to Planned Parenthood's own Harris Poll, only 28 percent of students surveyed were sexually active, and, of those who were, 80 percent felt they had been drawn into sexual activity too soon.[6] These were hardly the results Planned Parenthood had hoped for because the results are in direct opposition to everything they want children to believe. Therefore, they did their best to bury the results of their own survey and increased their efforts to put their version of sex-ed into the classroom, in hopes of getting children to change their minds.

Even the proponents of comprehensive sex-ed lack any evidence to prove its effectiveness. In fact, all existing documentation proves that rather than being the solution to sexual promiscuity and teen pregnancy, comprehensive sex-ed is part of the problem. Researchers from Johns Hopkins University stated that there is an "almost total absence of evidence" documenting any benefits of comprehensive sex-ed.[7] A study published in Planned Parenthood's own *Family Planning Perspectives* found that "prior exposure to a sex education course is positively and significantly associated with the initiation of sexual activity at ages 15 and 16."[8] It is vile and contemptible that Planned Parenthood continues to push comprehensive sex education on children *knowing* that doing so encourages early sexual activity.

Before the massive, federally subsidized intrusion of sex-ed into the classroom, teen pregnancy had steadily declined for more than a decade. The long decline quickly reversed itself once sex education became a staple in the public schools: In 1970, the pregnancy rate among seventeen- to nineteen-year-olds was sixty-eight per thousand. After ten years of comprehensive sex-ed, the rate jumped to ninety-six per thousand in 1980. In an effort to hide this miserable failure from the public, Planned Parenthood stopped quoting teen pregnancy rates, and, instead, began quoting statistics on falling birth rates. They failed to mention that the birth rate was not falling because of a drop in teen pregnancy—the birth rate was falling because of a greatly increased number of abortions. Between 1970 and 1987, the number of abortions increased by 250,000 even though the number of teenagers declined by four hundred thousand.[9] Currently, 40 percent of *all* teen pregnancies end in abortion.[10]

What Influences Sexual Behavior?

In a report requested by the U.S. Senate Committee on Labor and Human Resources, researchers determined that numerous factors determine whether or not a child becomes sexually involved at an early age. Because of the vast amount of time children spend watching television, media contributes to increased sexual activity among children because of the way sex is portrayed in T.V. and movies. Media seldom depicts any visible consequences for sexual involvement.[11] In addition, researchers believe peer pressure has a negative influence on the concept of sexual abstinence, largely because children don't want to be viewed as behaving "outside the norm." Because of the media portrayal and the way sex is presented through comprehensive sex-ed courses, some children actually believe "everyone does it."

Researchers found that future orientation also determines the degree of sexual activity or abstinence. Orientation is linked to the way a child envisions his options for the future and how he views himself: Am I attractive? Am I capable? Do I have desirable options in my life? Do I have a right to make my own choices and to determine what is right and wrong? Am I in control of myself and my destiny?

Because puberty comes before cognitive and emotional maturity, teens are physiologically capable of sexual activity before they are psychologically or socially prepared. This factor is known as Maturational Pace, and it also affects the child's choice regarding sexual activity.

The senate report also showed that activities influence sexual behavior. Early, frequent, and steady dating often lead to early sexual activity because those children have more opportunities for involvement. In addition, children who use drugs and alcohol at an early age or are truant or drop out of school are more prone to sexual promiscuity. The type of value system a child has is also a determining factor, so church involvement was an indicator in this category. It was found that children who are active in church are less likely to engage in promiscuous sexual behavior.

Parental and home factors also proved important. It was determined that children in single-parent families are more likely to be sexually active, as are children of mothers who were, themselves, sexually active during the preteen or teen-age years. Researchers determined that children with older, sexually active siblings are more likely to be sexually involved. The report also showed that sexual activity and pregnancy rates declined proportionate to the amount of communication and mutual trust between parent and child and inasmuch as parents stressed the value of abstinence and self-respect to their children.

The socioeconomic level, ethnic group, and age of children—known as Demographic Characteristics—also contribute to the variation in rates of sexual activity and pregnancy.[12]

Diagnosis of all these key elements is essential if we are to alter attitudes toward early sexual activity and address the subsequent problems of promiscuity, sexually transmitted diseases, and teen pregnancy. More than any other single factor, your child's *value system* will determine whether or not he or she becomes sexually active because the belief system determines the way all the other factors are *interpreted*. The idea that one can make informed decisions about sexual activity while being taught that morality is relative is absurd.

Always at issue is the question of what government has a right to do through the public education channel. As sex-ed exists today, government assumes to nurture children by force-feeding them a doctrine of humanism and moral relativism. It has never been the mandate of the United States government, *nor of public education*, to teach children what to think about sex. In their zeal to force humanism down the throats of America's youth, the state forgot to mention that there are alternative choices; immorality is constantly endorsed, but biblical morality is never even presented as an option worthy of consideration.

Entertaining Ideas

In addition to the textbook courses always associated with sex education, students are forced to participate in activities and exercises relative to that curriculum. For years, sex-ed "teacher" Suzi Landolphi has "entertained" students in public schools with a ninety-minute performance in which she simulates masturbation on stage using lewd, filthy language to communicate her viewpoints about various parts of the anatomy, orgasm, and bodily functions. Landolphi travels all over the country with her disgusting presentation and is paid quite handsomely with taxpayer's dollars.

Landolphi opens her "act" proclaiming: "What we're going to do is . . . have a group sexual experience here today. How's that? Is that good?" Because of her excessive vulgarity and salacious language, a group of irate students filed a $3.5 million dollar lawsuit against her claiming sexual harassment and a violation of rights to privacy and freedom of religion. With any luck, they'll win big.

Parents have a right to object to public schools that act as forums for filth. What can possibly be gained by allowing such a despicable, degenerate person access to our children? Every principal is responsible for what children are learning, and each must be held personally accountable for the speakers allowed to address them. It is inconceivable to think that the same educators who prohibit the presence of religious influences on their campuses find nothing wrong with the Uribes and Landolphis who are paid to verbally sexually violate children.

The Purpose of Sex Education

In 1964, Mary Calderone, then medical director of Planned Parenthood-World Population, became the primary cofounder of SIECUS. (Calderone's association with Planned Parenthood is worthy of note; it accounts for that organization's long-standing, continuing access to innocent children through the public school system.) The primary goal of SIECUS has always been mandatory sex education for grades kindergarten through twelfth. By its own admission, SIECUS encourages sexual activity in children. When questioned regarding her views on sexual experimentation, Calderone said that "adolescent sexual experimentation is not just inevitable, but actually *necessary for normal development*" (emphasis added).[13] According to Calderone, sex-ed should "separate children from their parents in order to give them a new, values-neutral sexual identity."[14]

Calderone's "Principles Basic to Education for Sexuality" was the blueprint for much of the sex-ed curriculum used in schools today—curriculum as lewd as any pornography most adults have ever seen or imagined. According to Calderone's own guidelines, "SIECUS supports the informed use of sexually explicit materials for educational . . . purposes" and "opposes legislative and judicial efforts to prevent the production and/or distribution of sexually explicit materials" to children.[15] It is inconceivable that someone allegedly looking out for the best interest of children would even *think* such a thing, let alone be bold enough to put such a diabolical opinion in print!

In the same report, Calderone lauds the merits of "self-pleasuring," emphasizing the "need" to teach masturbation as a "natural and nonharmful part of sexual behavior" for children of *all ages*.[16] Calderone views sexual experimentation in children as a "personal right" and says that "children of *all ages* have the capacity to establish caring, loving [sexual] relationships with people of *all ages*."[17] Presumably, she's referring to sex between adults and children.

It bears repeating that SIECUS—the Sex Information and Education Council of the United States—has been called "one of the most prestigious private educational groups in the country." (In all sincerity, I pray from my heart, "God, help us!")

SIECUS creates guidelines for sex-ed classes and approves curriculum. In SIECUS, we have a group of "prestigious" government agents who unabashedly declare that sexual experimentation in children is acceptable and necessary. Without shame or hesitation, SIECUS supports the use of pornographic materials "for educational . . . purposes" and actively opposes any efforts to stop the production and/or distribution of sexually explicit materials to children! By their own admission, SIECUS condones sexual relationships between children and adults and views homosexuality and the teaching of masturbation as perfectly acceptable.

When expressing her view on homosexuality, Calderone explained "sexual orientation" as a "fundamental human right" and stresses that "the majority of individuals have some elements of both homosexuality and heterosexuality in their makeup." In her report, Calderone claimed that homosexuality is "perfectly normal."[18] To prove her point (I guess), she proudly admits that she took part in a Sexual Attitudinal Reassessment program (sensitivity training) in which she viewed a homosexual couple keeping house and having sex—sodomizing each other. She reported in *US Catholic's Magazine* (October 1982) that the experience left her "walking on air" because she "knew what homosexuals did . . . and it was fine." In my opinion, Calderone is a sick individual, and she has no right teaching children *anything*—especially sex education! It is absolutely beyond belief that she—or anyone remotely like her—could hold a position of authority in which she can influence the morals of a generation. Even those who do not question an individual's right to promiscuous sex should certainly question the need to *teach* such perversity to innocent children.

Not surprisingly, SIECUS only endorses "values-neutral" curriculum that is "not concerned with the content of people's values, but the *process of valuing*."[19] Given the fact that SIECUS curriculum undermines the values of church and family, it is anything *but* neutral. By affirming the relativity of all values, the authors of such curricula push *their* belief system on all children. Indeed, any challenge from students or teachers with traditional moral values is usually met with disdain as the opponent is accused of moralizing, preaching, or being prudish. As one student said, "Planned Parenthood tolerates everything but good morals."

Here are some of the topics SIECUS is teaching our children and a (very brief) synopsis of the content of each. (PLEASE NOTE: The following information was taken *directly* from the most recent edition of the SIECUS publication, "Guidelines for Comprehensive Sexuality Education." Any parent who wants a copy can get one by writing SIECUS at 130 West 42nd Street, #2500, New York, NY 10036.) It's important to note that all topics are discussed at all age levels.

1. *Body image* teaches that: Bodies are different. All bodies are special. Good health habits can improve the way a body looks. A person's value is not determined by how they look. Bodies change during puberty. The size

and shape of the penis or breasts does not affect the ability to be a good sexual partner. A person who likes the way he or she looks will be more attractive to other people.

2. *Sexual identity and orientation* teaches that: Everyone is born a boy or a girl. Human beings experience different kinds of loving. Some men and women are heterosexual, and some are homosexual. Homosexual, heterosexual, and bisexual people are alike. Homosexual and bisexual people are "often mistreated, called hurtful names, or denied rights." Homosexual relationships can be as fulfilling as heterosexual relationships. "Gay men and lesbians can form families." Homosexual couples behave sexually in many of the same ways as heterosexual couples. "Many" young people "mainly feel attracted to their own gender"; this is perfectly acceptable. People do not choose their sexual orientation. Sexual orientation cannot be changed.

3. *Shared sexual behavior* teaches that: Adults express themselves by kissing, hugging, and engaging in other sexual behavior. Being sexual involves more than just sexual intercourse. Sexual relationships are enhanced when a couple communicates about what sexual behavior they like. A person has the right to refuse any sexual behavior. Some sexual expressions are prohibited by law and disapproved of by religious and cultural groups, but that doesn't mean such behaviors are wrong. Sexual behaviors include kissing, touching, caressing, massage, sharing erotic literature or art, bathing/showering together, and oral, vaginal, or anal intercourse.

All sex-ed curriculum sanctioned by SIECUS and Planned Parenthood contains all or most of the elements listed above, as directed by SIECUS through their guidelines. By using your imagination and remembering your own adolescence, it is not difficult to imagine the course that classroom conversations often take when these subjects are discussed. If your child is unfortunate enough to have a teacher who condones sexual perversity and promiscuity, the possibilities for disaster are endless. Typical sex-ed curriculum downgrades the affectionate, monogamous nature of human sexuality and equates sexual acts with self-gratification and lust. Sex-ed, as endorsed by SIECUS, teaches that it's perfectly normal for children to have sexual fantasies and that they have a right to fulfill those fantasies by expressing themselves sexually, whenever and wherever they feel it's appropriate. Sex-ed, as many children experience it, robs them of innocence and modesty and ignores the spiritual aspect of sexuality that comes when God joins two people together through marriage and blesses them with a sexual union through which to express how they love and cherish each other.

Pornography Disguised As Education

In his in-depth book titled *Grand Illusions: The Legacy of Planned Parenthood* (highly recommended reading), author George Grant cites example after example of child sexual abuse in the classroom where pure pornography masquerades as sex education, as children are forced to take part in "role-playing" that often proves humiliating and degrading. Some teens are required to view pornographic movies as part of the course. One young woman confessed that she had never seen a pornographic movie before and that it was "worse than what she could have imagined." She admitted that when the lights came back on the entire class seemed shocked by what they had seen. Then, the attractive representative from Planned Parenthood (who brought the film) began to soothe them, explaining that what they had just seen was "totally normal and totally good." Smiling sweetly, she then proceeded to pass out condoms, instructing the boys to "hold up a finger" so the girls could practice contraceptive application! The young woman relaying this experience told Mr. Grant that, afterwards, several of the girls began sobbing, one ran out of the room and threw up, and one fainted.

"I have never been more humiliated," the young lady said. "I felt dirty and defiled after seeing the film. . . . It was horrible. It was like I'd been raped."[20]

Planned Parenthood curricula and the activities associated with it are specifically designed to break down sexual inhibitions and undermine traditional values. Those who doubt Planned Parenthood's motives or philosophies are urged to call or visit a local chapter and request some literature for your teen-ager—just make sure that your teen-ager never sees it! Instead, read it yourself, and make your own determinations regarding the "value" of this billion dollar adversary to the family, euphemistically called Planned Parenthood.

The Curriculum

The content of sex education materials used in many schools today would disgust any responsible adult, given the fact that the material is aimed at children. The books are replete with four-letter words, total nudity, and intimate details of sexual encounters and perversities, often as told by the children who experienced them. Cartoons show naked characters making slang references to their body parts. Next to drawings which show genitals from every conceivable position are lists of filthy slang words for sexual organs and functions. (No reference is made as to why Planned Parenthood feels this information is vital or why valuable class time should be used to discuss it.) Instructions for using feminine hygiene products are graphically illustrated, as are ways to use vaginal foams and put on a condom. This stuff would be embarrassing enough in segregated classrooms, but the fact that the courses are offered coed is repugnant.

Textbooks describing intimate sexual intercourse and its resultant physiological effects on various parts of the human anatomy reads like pornography. The presentation of this material, while highly unnecessary in the first place, is diabolical in its attempt to arouse the students who read it. The following text would disturb many adults if it were read in the context of adult books or magazines; it is even more disturbing to think that this pornography is given to young children by their teachers. In order to emphasize the dire problem with sex-ed curriculum, I took the risk of offending some readers. Following are a few examples, *quoted verbatim*, from classroom textbooks—and, believe me, these are *not* the worst examples I could find.*

> I have fantasies just about every night. . . . I lie there with all these sexy things going on in my head, and of course my hand always seems to make it down to my ——.[21]

For sixth through eighth grade students, Planned Parenthood proudly recommends *Boys and Sex* and *Girls and Sex*, both written by Wardell Pomeroy. Pomeroy is a former colleague of Alfred Kinsey and coauthor of the Kinsey report. There are those who have little doubt that Kinsey, Pomeroy, and their colleagues sexually molested children as part of their "research." In an article titled "A New Look at Incest" (*Forum* publication's *Variations*, 1977), Pomeroy shared his belief that "incest between adults and younger children can . . . prove to be a satisfying and enriching experience."

In *Boys and Sex*, Pomeroy tells eleven-year-olds that "boys who live on farms . . . have intercourse with animals . . . [Some] build a strong emotional attachment to a particular animal . . . a loving sexual relationship." Besides endorsing bestiality, Pomeroy gives children instruction in the mechanics of sexual intercourse which (I'm absolutely serious) includes information on how to

---

*The editors at Huntington contemplated printing the entire excerpt furnished by the author, but they ultimately decided that some of the content was too graphic and offensive for publication—even though it originally appeared in a school textbook.

"increase the frequency of ejaculation" and how to have sex "doggie fashion."[22] In many school districts, children are *required* to read this smut!

In *Love and Sex In Plain Language*, the author makes the astute observation that "it's really impossible to masturbate too much because when your body has had enough it will no longer respond to such efforts to have an orgasm."[23]

Changing Bodies, Changing Lives lauds the merits of mutual masturbation as a perfect way of "giving each other pleasure without worrying about pregnancy."[25] The text is extremely explicit and leaves absolutely nothing to the imagination; every conceivable four-letter word is used. The section subtitled "Having Sexual Intercourse" is more than a page in length and reads like the script from a hard-core porno movie. Later, in the same chapter, the section titled "Learning about Sex with Someone Else" gives step-by-step instructions and even devotes a couple of pages to "Making Lovemaking Better." (How considerate of Planned Parenthood!)

Changing Bodies, Changing Lives begins exploration of homosexuality by telling teens that "many people have one or a few homosexual experiences"[26] and continues to perpetuate the lie that "about 10 percent, are mainly attracted to people of their own sex." Again, the text is replete with graphic descriptions of homosexual encounters between preteen and teen-age children and sometimes between children and adults, and the experiences are always relayed as positive. The authors give homosexual students instructions on how to ease the pain of "coming out" and also describe, in detail, the various ways in which homosexuals have sexual intercourse.

In addition to arousing sexual curiosity and removing inhibitions, values-neutral sex-ed material is designed to alienate children from their parents. In an effort to make kids who don't share their view feel abnormal, *Changing Bodies, Changing Lives* makes continual reference to "most teens." Planned Parenthood claims "most teens" in *their* surveys "spend much less time at home" with their parents and that "most teens" feel "equipped to take on the full responsibility of adulthood." In other words, they don't need parents telling them what to do. Then, they go on to interview "Alexandra"—*a seventh grade child!*[27] The text implies that if the reader enjoys being home with his parents and is not ready to be on his own, he's somehow a freak of nature. Parents are consistently presented as well-meaning, old-fashioned nerds, sadly ill-equipped to deal with the problems of adolescence which their wiser, more worldly children are experiencing. So, the authors suggest that "if it seems that your parents are holding on too tightly, you may feel you have to push them away, shouting 'You never let me do anything!' "[28]

And, certainly no sex-ed textbook endorsed by Planned Parenthood and SIECUS would be complete without a photograph of a teen-age girl blowing up a condom,[29] nor could one expect Planned Parenthood to distribute textbooks that do not include information on where and how to gain access to the contraceptives and abortions which are such a lucrative part of their business.

The only way to determine whether your district is using any of the texts above, or others equally as bad, is to ask. Some districts allow students to "opt-out" of these courses, but many do not. Even when the option exists, some students will not opt-out for fear of being made fun of if they do.

Teaching Abstinence: Proven Effective

The University of South Carolina promotes a program in which participants agree to postpone sexual involvement. In that community, the number of virgins among seventeen-year-old black females has risen from 38 percent to 58 percent during a four-year period, contrasted to a 32 percent average in the comparison community.

Abstinence-based (SIECUS calls it "fear-based") cur-

riculum is the only curriculum proven effective in slow-
ing sexual activity among teens, yet many educators fear
teaching abstinence-only, because of lawsuits brought by
the ACLU charging that abstinence-only curriculum violates a student's right to choose sexual activity. (Does the
same child have the right to be protected from exposure
to sexual perversity and pornography? Where is the ACLU
when students with traditional moral values are being
violated by curricula which encourage promiscuity that
places them physically and emotionally at risk?) Abstinence curricula alert children to the dangers and illusions
of peer pressure and encourage them to make right and
moral choices. If Planned Parenthood or the ACLU sincerely cared about children, they would encourage the
teaching of abstinence-only curriculum—instead, they fight
it in court.

    Recently, the Department of Health and Human Ser-
vices (HHS) issued a report in which it determined that
"a significantly higher percentage of students who received abstinence instruction remained virgins, compared
to students that did not."[30] The study, which was done in
partnership with the Utah-based Institute for Research
and Evaluation, tested three abstinence-only curricula:
"Teen Aid," "Sex Respect," and "Values and Choices."
Interestingly, "Sex Respect"—the course with the strongest abstinence message—was the most successful in reducing teen pregnancy; the least successful of the three
was "Values and Choices," which, of the three, offered
the most watered-down approach to teaching abstinence.[31]
Following the study, though they wouldn't admit failure,
the HHS *did* admit that values-neutral sex-ed courses
wrongly define the problem because they're aimed at
reducing pregnancy instead of preventing sexual activity.
Apparently, no one at HHS was intelligent enough to
interpret their own study because no one from that agency
suggested the obvious. That is that current methods of
teaching sex-ed are an abject failure, and change must
occur.

According to the HHS report, biological sex-ed approaches (like distributing condoms) are *least effective* in influencing teen sexual behavior. In order of importance, here are the five major factors as teens determined them:

1. *Value System:* The sense of what is good and bad, right and wrong. (This sort of shoots holes through the argument for values-neutral courses.)
2. *Social System:* Significant others who influence them. (Certainly, teachers fall into this category!)
3. *Related Risk Factors:* Drug or alcohol use, early dating, etc.
4. *Personality Traits:* Is the student a natural risk-taker?
5. *Informational System:* How much do they know about sex, sexuality and reproduction?[32]

Students listed moral values as the number-one factor influencing their sexual behavior. Therefore, any sex-ed curriculum or program that hopes to curb teen pregnancy or sexual activity *must* begin by teaching sex-ed within the confines of traditional morality. Of the students participating in the study, 22.4 percent were sexually active, as opposed to 37 percent in the group not taking the abstinence course—a difference of almost 15 percent. Quite surprisingly, researchers found that the abstinence approach works best with students who begin the course with permissive sexual attitudes. Those students proved highly likely to experience a value shift. Upon completion of the course, a significant number of sexually active teens made the decision, on their own, to abstain. Understandably, the HHS study (done in the fall of 1992) has never been widely released—most likely because the results offer indisputable proof that public education's current approach to sex education and public health issues is unequivocally wrong.

As the positive results of abstinence-based sex-ed are becoming known, several states have mandated that public school sex-ed programs must be abstinence-based. Programs designed to help kids stop having sex also exist.

Though it's too early to measure long-term results, the initial results are impressive.[33]

In her excellent report "Has Sex Education Failed Our Teenagers?" Dr. Dinah Richard cites the following statement:

> The time has come to stop blaming the problems of teen pregnancy [and promiscuity] on the incorrigibility of our children or the ills of society. Our children have only *us* for guidance; and we are responsible for the condition of our society. The real path back to a sane and effective policy . . . does not circumvent the family, but leads straight to the heart of it. It encourages communication between parents and children and is built on the firm foundation of parents' values, beliefs, and ambitions for their children.[34]

That statement, surprisingly written by members of the U.S. House Select Committee on Children, Youth, and Families, is eloquent and true. Where were these statesmen when Goals 2000 was being voted on? Where are they now that the U.N. Convention of the Rights of the Child is threatening to destroy the American family? And, why aren't they acting against this heinous sexual assault on our children? Clearly, those currently making public education policy and designing curricula do not share the philosophy of the authors of that statement.

Though abstinence programs are proven effective, the directive to "just say no" brings with it the implication of moral absolutes—a concept not accepted by organizations like the NEA and SIECUS, primarily responsible for the creation and distribution of sex-ed material. When publicly funded, most sex-ed curricula mention abstinence only within the context of contraceptive options. While the value of teaching abstinence has been clearly seen, even in Third-World countries, our policy-makers ignore it, probably because (from Planned Parenthood's perspective) there's no money to be made on sexually abstinent teenagers.

Uganda had the highest rate of HIV infection in Africa until Dr. S.I. Okware, the director of Uganda's AIDS Control Program, finally had enough. He went to the media and public schools and churches, demanding that all begin to teach AIDS education programs based on moral precepts. Okware insisted that all government employees be educated about the disease and its moral implications. Further, the president of Uganda refused to pass out condoms to children, stating his belief that doing so "would send the wrong message to the youth of Uganda." "Condoms tell our youth," he said, "that promiscuity is all right. Our program . . . is to encourage morality, and our program is working."[37] Dr. Okware now reports that incidents of sexually transmitted diseases reported to area clinics fell from an average of ten to fifteen per day, per clinic, to "one per week, if that." Obviously, Dr. Okware has more common sense than anyone making public health policy in the United States.

For years, secular humanists have equated our children with animals by suggesting they can't possibly control their sexual urges. Surgeon General Joycelyn Elders insists that we can stop teens from smoking but says we can't stop them from having sex. Our kids deserve more credit than that, and they deserve to live in a society that doesn't lower its standards to accommodate promiscuity. Anyone who hears a lie long enough will eventually come to believe it. Because our kids have been told they can't control their sexual urges, they've come to accept that lie as truth. The ability to think rationally and then make responsible decisions is the thing that separates humans from animals. Self-control is a trait unique to humans and, as such, is a mere matter of engaging the will. If the desire is present, the will can be directed and emotions can be controlled. The challenge lies in giving kids a reason to desire purity.

In an ideal world, children would choose to remain

pure because purity pleases God and their parents; for some teens, that is motivation enough. But, unfortunately, many kids today have no spiritual priorities because they're being taught that God does not exist and that they are in control of their own destinies. Consequently, children feel responsible only to themselves and fear no consequences for their behavior. Generally speaking, kids worry about the present—getting their immediate needs met and gratifying their own selfish desires; they don't think much about the future, let alone an afterlife. There is a void in every human heart, and, if God doesn't fill it, something destructive will. Children are having sex during childhood because they're spiritually empty and, many times, emotionally abandoned by parents too busy with their own careers to notice that their children need them.

Television and movies, publications and music, and a liberal dominant media are filling minds that should be thriving on wholesome literature and moral ideals with the idea that promiscuity is the norm and multiple sexual conquests, the ideal. The idea that one should respect oneself and others has been replaced with the idea that pleasing oneself is the most important thing. Media dictates that anything is permissible, and those who don't go along with the "new morality" are an out-of-step minority who will not be accepted by their peers.

More than anything, kids want to be accepted. They want to feel as though they are part of the group—even if the group is wrong. Hidden beneath a child's need to feel accepted is the deeper need to feel safe. In spite of how they act, all children want and need boundaries. When public education began to teach that there are no moral absolutes, government infringed on the safe boundaries of morality set by the church and traditional family and left our kids to free-fall into the immoral quagmire that exists today. Our failure to set limits by defining right and wrong has sent society into a tailspin.

Parents must demand that schools replace all pornographic sex-ed material with sex-ed courses based upon moral precepts. Beginning today, children must be told the truth about the physical and emotional consequences resulting from selfish, promiscuous sex. Our kids must be told they can, and should, control themselves because they are important and valuable to us and because they deserve self-respect and a chance to live life; we don't want their lives shortened by the deadly HIV infection or emotionally destroyed by sexual promiscuity or unwanted pregnancy. If SIECUS, the NEA, the government, or Planned Parenthood cared at all about children, the fact that promiscuity can kill them would be incentive enough for them to finally tell the truth.

Because those with private agendas have told parents that "kids are gonna do it" no matter what they say, parents have shirked their responsibility to teach the value of chastity. In a time when promiscuity is broadcast as "normal," children who remain chaste are almost always labeled "abnormal." Further, parents who would never hand their own child a condom are quietly and passively allowing public schools to do it for them. The fact is no politician or government agency, no member of the National Education Association, no member of the homosexual community or Planned Parenthood loves your child. Therefore, it's not only ridiculous, but dangerous, to allow them to dictate morality to the children you love and cherish. Parents have got to stop government from dictating morality to their children; they've got to take a stand against values-neutral courses that endorse promiscuity and perversion. We need to save our children from government run amuck in the same way that we'd snatch them from the path of an oncoming train. We must protect our children from Planned Parenthood's agenda in the same way that we protect them from child molesters and pedophiles.

Abstinence-based Curricula

Following is a list of known directive, abstinence-based

curricula. This is an incomplete list; there are many others. None of the courses listed have been studied in depth nor are any specifically endorsed by the author; the list is meant to provide a starting point for research should your district want to implement an abstinence-only course.

Grade School:
Learning About Myself and Others (Lamo)
(Privately funded; no government funds.)

Elementary School:
Responsible Social Values Program (sixth through eighth grade)

Junior High:
Teen Choice: Reasonable Reasons to Wait
Art of Loving Well
Challenge Program
Me, My World, My Future
F.A.C.T.S.
Choosing the Best (Privately funded.)
Love and Life (Privately funded.)
God Made You Unique (Grades five through twelve. Privately funded.)

High School:
Anchor
Facing Reality
Sexuality, Commitment and Family
AIDS (HIV) You Can Live Without It
F.A.C.T.S.
Drinking, Drugs & Sex: A Reason to Say No (Video. Privately funded.)
God Made You Unique (Grades five through twelve. Privately funded.)

The Price of Innocence

No organization has done more to destroy the morals of this nation's children than Planned Parenthood. In the absence of sexual promiscuity, that organization could not exist. Thus, their motive for encouraging sexual activity in children at a younger and younger age is explained. Arguing that every dollar "invested in family planning" (given to them) would "save two or three dollars in health and welfare costs," Planned Parenthood convinced government to invest billions of dollars in programs that encourage promiscuity. By claiming government entitlements and overcharging those who qualify for those programs, they make hundreds of millions of dollars annually at taxpayer's expense.[38]

The largest provider of abortions in the world,[39] Planned Parenthood boasts of murdering 132,314 babies in the womb in 1992. At an average cost of about $325 each, that's more than $43 million for abortions—a large portion of their total $500 million annual income.[40] According to their 1992 Annual Report, they made about $150 million on clinic services—largely from the sale of condoms and birth control pills.

In addition to their considerable contributions in the area of teaching our children how to have sex, Planned Parenthood has done more than any other "straight" organization to advance prohomosexual curricula in schools. In return for their efforts on behalf of homosexuals, that group has taken an active prochoice stance to aid Planned Parenthood. Homosexual groups make large financial contributions to Planned Parenthood which, in turn, creates sex-ed curricula that is unquestionably prohomosexual. And around and around it goes.

Planned Parenthood actively fights against any curriculum that endorses traditional morality by challenging those programs in court. Abstinence-only curricula, like Sex Respect and Teen Aid, teach students that the only certain way to prevent pregnancy, STDs, and AIDS is not to have sex. The fact that both programs discourage sex before marriage really bothers Planned Parenthood. Even though the Supreme Court ruled that federal funding for

abstinence programs was not a violation of the Establishment Clause, Planned Parenthood managed to get restraining orders against those curricula in a few school
districts by convincing local courts that the courses were
"religious."

Though anyone with two brain cells knows that, if
you don't have sex, you don't get pregnant or contract
AIDS, Planned Parenthood doesn't want teens to know
that abstinence could save their lives and the lives of all
the babies whose tiny, fully formed bodies are found in
dumpsters outside of their abortion clinics. It's inconceivable that any rational woman would endorse or support
an organization that makes millions of dollars annually by
exploiting women through abortion. The same feminist
activists, who profess to care so much about making things
better for generations of women to come, are ignoring
the fact that half of the babies murdered in the womb
each year are female.

What Government Research Proves

Dr. Stan E. Weed, president of the Institute for Research and Evaluation, and Joseph A. Olsen are the researchers recently contracted to submit a report on teen
pregnancy prevention to the U.S. Senate Committee of
Labor and Human Resources. The report was designed
to help policy makers formulate appropriate and effective
public policy to prevent teen pregnancy. Not surprisingly,
the report found that

> the primary cause of teen pregnancy, has . . . received
> the least attention. . . . If . . . we see pregnancies to
> unwed teens as premature, then one might just as
> easily view the sexual activity leading to that preg-
> nancy as premature. As much as one might like to,
> there simply is no way of separating teen pregnancy
> from premature sexual activity [emphasis added].[41]

The report studied numerous sex-ed curricula, focusing on three strategies of sex education: Traditional sex-ed, "comprehensive" sex-ed (contraceptive counseling and services for teens), and prevention of early sexual activity (abstinence). The report concluded that "one of the striking features of all [three] efforts is the general lack of independent, systematic evaluation of program outcomes and intended results" and, further, that much of what is being done "is being done on the basis of deeply held *but untested assumptions*" (emphasis added).[42]

Traditional sex-ed assumes that children, given enough information, will act responsibly and, thus, lower the risk of pregnancy. After looking at countless traditional courses and evaluating data from agencies hired to study them, researchers reported that those programs, though they increase knowledge, have "little direct impact on values and attitudes, actual sexual behavior, use of birth control, and teenage pregnancy." Further, they found that "exposure to a course appears to be associated with a slightly *increased* probability of subsequent sexual activity among [teens]." In summary, they determined that "requiring students to take more sex education, as it is currently provided, is *not* the answer" (emphasis added).[43]

Comprehensive sex-ed assumes that sexual activity among children is a given, that the behavior cannot be changed, and that protecting children from the consequences of their actions will reduce the risks of sexual activity. This ridiculous assumption is most assuredly made by the same people who deny the benefits of teaching cognitive skills. Obviously, those who continue to make this assumption have not thought the issue through rationally: If children know there are no consequences for wrong behavior, what will possibly motivate them to *change* wrong behavior?

Using data from all fifty states, Weed and Olsen assessed the impact and effectiveness of comprehensive sex-ed. They found a reduction in births of eighty per one thousand, but there was an increase in pregnancies of

forty per one thousand and a 120 per one thousand
increase in abortions.[44] The researchers obviously concluded that the assumption that comprehensive sex-ed
causes a reduction in teen pregnancy rates "is not consistent with the evidence."[45] Indeed, if such programs were
at all effective, teen pregnancy would have decreased proportionate to enrollment in the courses. As further expla-
nation of why such programs will not work, the report
notes the teen's inherent "lack of developmental capacity
and maturity to engage in the rational decision-making
process." Also noted are the adolescent's natural tendencies toward egocentrism, impulsivity, immediacy, risk-tak-
ing, and "a constricted sense of what the future may
hold."

Abstinence-based sex-ed correctly and logically assumes
that the only way to eliminate teen pregnancy is to admit
that sexual activity is the cause and then proceed to give
children guidance and instruction in ways to say "NO!"

Weed and Olsen point out that "socioeconomic as
well as public health concerns underscore the importance
of addressing abstinence as a public policy issue."[46] They
note that "sexual abstinence has been treated . . . as a moral
issue, and people have been reluctant to make public
policy simply on the basis of morality."[47] One must pause
to wonder why telling children *not* to have sex is considered "moralizing," but teaching them *how* to have sex is
not.

The Adolescent Family Life Act (Title XX) legislation
directly addresses the issue of teaching sexual abstinence.
Though not supported by SIECUS or Planned Parenthood, and not seen as a credible solution to teen pregnancy by proponents of school-based clinics, the federally
funded program is an attempt to intervene before sexual
activity begins. It states, in part,

> The prevention of adolescent sexual activity and
> adolescent pregnancy depends primarily upon de-
> veloping strong family values and close family ties;
> and since the family is the basic social unit in

which the values and attitudes . . . concerning sexuality . . . are formed, programs designed to deal with issues of sexuality and pregnancy will be successful to the extent that such programs encourage and sustain the role of the family in dealing with adolescent sexual activity and . . . pregnancy.[48]

Evaluation of the demonstration projects associated with Title XX has proved that it is possible to realize a significant shift in values and attitudes about sexuality.

In summary, the Weed/Olsen study found that, based on all available evidence:

1) Sexual activity among children is not inevitable, irreversible, or desirable.

2) Knowledge alone is an inadequate basis for behavior changes. In order to be effective, sex-ed must deal with belief and value systems and decision-making skills.

3) Teen attitudes about sex are part of a broader, significant set of beliefs about human life, dignity, and relationships, and the family as a key unit of society. Sex-ed programs must deal with sexuality in that broader context.

4) Parents *must* reinforce what is taught "by communicating their own beliefs."

5) "Abstinence is the preferred approach" and when "properly presented, it will be seen as a viable, practical, and preferred choice by teens."

6) "Teens are confused" by messages that teach "abstinence is best, but contraception works for those who do not choose abstinence."

A report from the National Research Council, "Risking the Future," further suggests that "new approaches to encourage the delay of sexual intercourse should be designed, implemented, and evaluated." The Weed/Olsen study determined that programs based on parental involvement and a values-based approach to sexual activity—with a primary emphasis on abstinence—is the key to prevention of teen pregnancies. Still, SIECUS, the NEA, and Planned Parenthood ignore the advice of these experts, continuing, instead, to teach children how to have sex and how to use contraceptives in order to "protect themselves" from the consequences.

Parents must be bold in presenting the facts contained in the research cited and must take a firm stand to implement abstinence-only sex-ed curricula in schools throughout America. Using the research cited as the example, we must alert educators to the value and positive results acquired from teaching children the value of self-respect and delayed gratification. We must make a commitment to implement action and to stand firm until sex-ed curriculum based on moral precepts is taught in our local schools.

Endnotes

1. Gary F. Kelly, *Learning About Sex* (Hauppauge, N.Y.: Barron's Educational Series, Inc., 1986), 60-61.

2. George Grant and Mark A. Horne, *Legislating Immorality* (Chicago: Moody Press, 1993), 74.

3. Dr. Melvin Anchell, "Sexologists on the Couch: Psychoanalysis vs. Sex Education," *National Review* (20 June 1986): 33-38.

4. Ibid., 38.

5. Ibid., 60.

6. Lewis Harris and Associates, The Planned Parenthood Poll: "American Teens Speak: Sex, Myths, TV and Birth Control" (New York, 1986).

7. Melvin Zelnik and Young J. Kim, "Sex Education and its Association with Teenage Sexual Activity, Pregnancy, and Contraceptive Use," *Family Planning Perspectives* (May/June 1982): 118.

8. "The Controversy Over Sex Education," *In Focus*, Family Research Council report.

9. Thomas Sowell, "The Big Lie," *Forbes* (23 December 1991): 52.

10. Vital Statistics of the United States, National Center for Health Statistics.

11. Stan E. Weed and Joseph A. Olsen, "Policy and Program Considerations for Teenage Pregnancy Prevention: A Summary for Policymakers." The article, based on a report submitted under contract to the U.S. Senate Committee on Labor and Human Resources, appeared in *Family Perspective Magazine* (vol. 22, no. 3): 245.

12. Ibid., 243-247.

13. Claire Chambers, "The SIECUS Circle, a Humanist Revolution" (Belmont, Mass.: Western Islands, 1977), 15.

14. Leonard Gross, "Sex Education Comes of Age," *Look Magazine* (8 March 1966).

15. *Education Reporter* (January 1992).

16. Mary S. Calderone, "The SIECUS/NYU Principles Basic to Education for Sexuality," the SIECUS Report, January, 1980, The Sex Information and Education Council of the U.S., Inc., New York.

17. Ibid.

18. Ibid.

19. Sidney B. Simon, Leland W. Howe and Howard Kirschenbaum, *Values Clarification, A Handbook for Practical Strategies for Teachers and Students*, rev. ed., (Glidden, Wisc.: Hart Publishing Co., Inc., 1978), 18-19.

20. George Grant, *Grand Illusions: The Legacy Of Planned Parenthood* (Franklin, Tenn.: Adroit Press, 1992), 109-110.

21. Ruth Bell et al, *Changing Bodies, Changing Lives*, rev. ed. (New York: Vintage, 1987), 16.

22. Wardell Pomeroy, *Boys and Sex* (New York: Delacourt Press, 1971), 127.

23. Eric W. Johnson, *Love And Sex in Plain Language*, 3d rev. ed. (New York: Bantam Books, 1989), 66.

24. Ibid.

25. Ibid., 115.

26. Ibid., 42.

27. Ibid., 43.

28. Ibid., 174.

29. Peter LaBarbera, "Teens Go for Abstinence," *Family Voice* (March 1993): 4.

30. Ibid., 5.

31. Ibid., 7.

32. Glen C. Griffin, M.D., "Condoms and Contraceptives in Junior High and High School Clinics: What do you think?" *Postgraduate Medicine* vol. 93, no. 5 (April 1993): 5.

33. The U.S. House Select Committee on Children, Youth, and Families, "Teen Pregnancy: What is Being Done? A State-by-State Look," as cited by Dr. Dinah Richard in her report, "Has Sex Education Failed Our Teenagers?" (Focus on the Family Publishing, 1990), 65.

34. Stanley Monteith, M.D., *AIDS: The Unnecessary Epidemic* (Sevierville, Tenn.: Covenant House Books, 1992), 80.

35. Planned Parenthood Federation of America, Inc., 1992 Service Report.

36. Grant, *Grand Illusions*, 23.

37. Ibid.

38. Stan E. Weed and Joseph A. Olsen, "Policy and Program Considerations for Teenage Pregnancy Prevention: A Summary for Policymakers." The article, based on a report submitted under contract to the U. S. Senate Committee on Labor and Human Resources, appeared in *Family Perspective Magazine*, vol. 22, no. 3, 237.

39. Ibid.

40. Ibid., 238.

41. Ibid., 239.

42. Ibid., 240.

43. Ibid., 242.

44. Ibid.

45. Sec. 2001, the Public Health Service Act, Title XX, paragraph 10A.

School-based Health Clinics

Flee from sexual immorality. All other sins a man commits are outside his body, but he who sins sexually sins against his own body.

—1 Corinthians 6:18

We've taught kids what to do in the front seat of a car; now we've got to teach them what to do in the back seat.

—Surgeon General Joycelyn Elders, defending her position to give condoms to children

Government spends more than $2 billion annually on Title X "family planning" programs designed to prevent teen pregnancy and the spread of sexually transmitted diseases.[1] Based on the assumption that school-based clinics (SBCs) will slow the rate of teen pregnancy, SBCs received about 450 million of those dollars in 1993.[2] The Center for Population Control is the government agency most involved in the drive to place SBCs on campuses across America, despite the fact that "there was no substantial decline in pregnancy or birthrates among . . . students in schools with clinics."[3] In just five years (1989-1993), the number of government-subsidized health clinics on public school campuses has increased from 5 to 325.[4] Inasmuch as the Goals 2000 albatross mandates "access to appropriate social services [and] health care," we can expect to see hundreds more of these clinics popping up all across the country.

More than five thousand family planning clinics in America give contraceptives and abortion referrals to a million and a half teens each year, and that number continues to grow. *Education Newsline* (May/June 1994) reports that Oregon governor Barbara Roberts wants to double the number of SBCs in her state.[5] The main difference between school-based and family planning clinics is their physical proximity to children. The irony of SBCs is that they were created because existing family planning clinics "weren't doing the job" in preventing teen pregnancies![6] In typical government fashion, politicians decided to fund more of what never worked in the first place.

Proponents say that SBCs must exist because many students can't afford health care. The ideal SBC "is a comprehensive, holistic, and multi-disciplinary health service specializing in the physical, emotional, and psychosocial needs of adolescents."[7] The rationale is simple, proponents say: "bring the doctor to the patient."

The point must be made here that Hillary Clinton is lying when she bemoans the number of people without health care; no one in the United States is without health care. Anyone can receive treatment from a government-subsidized facility if they do not have the means to pay. A few months ago, as Hillary was furiously pitching the need for socialized medicine in America, a van full of illegal aliens crashed on a highway in California. All eleven occupants were taken to the local hospital for treatment, and California taxpayers picked up the tab. Everyone is familiar with the stories of immigrants who come to this country to give birth, allowing the newborn child "free" medical care and welfare benefits for the rest of his life.

And, everyone's heard stories of the countless number of hoodlums injured in gang-related incidents all across America, who are given medical treatment at taxpayer expense—often running into the hundreds of thousands of dollars. As one Congressman so aptly said, "If Americans think they're paying a lot for health care now, just wait until it's 'free!'"

Even if the issue of SBCs was as simple as giving athletic physicals and flu shots, many would still question the burden on schools to provide health services. Concern over the health issues of students can sap educators of time, resources, and energy already stretched to the limit. But, the issue of SBCs on public school campuses goes much further than that. Apart from giving medical treatment to children, government assumes the right, this time through SBCs, to invade the privacy of its citizens by making itself the moral guardian of America. Instead of leaving families alone and letting parents instill values in their own children, government is attempting to undermine the rights of parents by interfering where it doesn't belong. Any child who walks into one of these clinics can get contraceptives and abortion referrals—usually, without parental notification or permission. Though the state denies that the primary purpose of SBCs is to dispense contraceptives and family planning advice, the Consortium on Educational Policy's study on SBCs reports that, of the twenty-three services performed by SBCs nationwide, fifteen have to do with reproductive services.[8]

For the most part, a student who goes to a school clinic with a sore throat will be sent to the doctor; most clinics aren't equipped to do things like throat cultures. But, they are equipped with microscopes for wet mounts and incubators for cultures of genital discharges. SBCs don't dispense antibiotics, but many are equipped to surgically insert contraceptive implants, and almost all give pregnancy tests and pelvic examinations—often without parental knowledge or consent. (Ironically, if a child gets a stress-related headache following her visit to the clinic, she must get permission from her mother to take an aspirin.) Counseling is also added to the list of "services" the government wants to give our children. Clinicians are always available to "talk about problems"—like what kind of birth control the child should use or, if it's too late, how to schedule an abortion without her parents finding out.

Proponents insist that parental permission is always a prerequisite for receiving family planning services. In a small number of cases, that is true. But, even if it were true in *all* cases, the same children who forge their parent's signatures on report cards and detention notices will do likewise when trying to secure contraceptives. If permission forms are used at all, the information on them is usually so vague that most parents would not suspect that the distribution of contraceptives and abortion referrals is part of the clinic's "services." Proponents also fail to admit that many parents are tricked into giving "permission by omission"; in other words, the school assumes permission because the parent has failed to write a letter to the contrary. Sadly, given the hectic pace of families today, the high frequency of single-parent households and working mothers, and the common lack of communication between teens and adults, it's altogether possible that a parent could go through life not even knowing that a school-based clinic exists on the campus! Another thing proponents won't tell parents is that once a child is inside the clinic, parents have absolutely no rights.[9]

Clinics *do* offer athletic physicals and general health assessments, but the focus of school-based clinics is clearly on reproductive services. In 1985, the Center for Population Options issued a report advising that "when a student comes to the clinic ostensibly for other reasons, the clinic can take that opportunity to see if the student wants to discuss sexual behavior and birth control."[10] School-based clinics, conjointly with the government's idea of sex-ed, are creating a promiscuous generation, the likes of which we have never seen. Since the opening of the first school-based clinic in 1970, illegitimate birth rates have increased by 36 percent.[11] Almost without exception, wherever SBCs have existed, sexual promiscuity has increased, as have the number of teen pregnancies and abortions.

In August 1986, *Education Reporter* announced that "providing tax-payer funded contraceptives and abortions to teenagers is leading to an increase . . . in teen pregnancies." The same report presented indisputable evidence that restrictions on clinic access and requirements for parental consent *are* effective in reducing pregnancy among teens. By way of example, when South Dakota reduced its use of Title X family planning funds for contraceptives and abortions, the pregnancy rate dropped. Likewise, when Minnesota made parental notification mandatory for minors seeking abortions, "there ensued dramatic reductions in abortions, births, and pregnancies."[12]

A 1980 study showed that the four states spending the most tax dollars on publicly funded abortions and birth control, all had "higher-than-average teenage pregnancy rates as well as higher-than-average rates of teenage abortions-plus-unmarried births."[13] Conversely, states that spend the *least* to fund free family planning services have the lowest rates of abortions-plus-unmarried births.[14] Dr. Jacqueline Kasun, who conducted the study, admits that "facts . . . suggest that [free abortion and contraceptive] programs create problems." As proof, she cites the state of California, which had consistently spent more than twice the national average on government-subsidized birth control. Later, officials were left to justify that policy in the face of a teenage pregnancy rate 30 percent higher than the national average and an abortion rate 60 percent higher. (To its credit, California recognized the failure of its policy and now mandates abstinence-based sex education—though parents must still be cautious in monitoring the curriculum their districts are using. Some courses teach "Say 'no,' but if you say 'yes,' be safe and use a condom." That vacillation is confusing to kids and falsely suggests that they can't get pregnant or contract STDs or AIDS if they use a condom. Further, some abstinence-based programs condone mutual masturbation as a way "of feeling good without risking pregnancy," and many are prohomosexual.)

Examining the Need of SBCs

Though the number of teen pregnancies continues to rise with the number of SBCs, Planned Parenthood (presumably) still doesn't get it. They're constantly bemoaning the need for *more* "family planning" on campus—and, of course, more tax dollars to pay for it.

According to their annual report, Planned Parenthood made $150,900,000 on clinic income and more than $43 million on abortions in 1992. (They admitted to butchering 132 thousand babies in the womb at about $325 each, compared to making 7,600 "adoption referrals"; one can see why it's in Planned Parenthood's best interest to keep children sexually active.) Clinics are failing for the same reason that sex-ed is failing: clinics do nothing to address the real problem, which is sexual promiscuity, but they do plenty to perpetuate it.

Proponents and liberal politicians justify the "need" for school-based clinics based on Planned Parenthood's propaganda, which falsely assumes that all kids are going to have sex so they need contraceptives in order to "be responsible." And, as with sex-ed, those proponents insist that clinics be morally neutral. Thus, a child going to a school-based clinic to "talk about problems" will never be told that sex outside of marriage is wrong. Though proponents insist that "abstinence is a central part of the sexual-counseling process,"[15] that is, quite simply, a blatant lie.

A Harris Poll, paid for by Planned Parenthood, showed that almost half of eighteen-year-old girls were virgins, and 20 percent of all those who listed themselves as "sexually active" had only had sex once. (The Department of Health and Human Services did a similar survey, reporting that 65 percent of girls under the age of eighteen, were not sexually active.) The Harris Poll also found that educating children about contraception is linked to higher levels of sexual activity, a discovery that completely rejects the presupposition that the more contraceptive information kids have, the more responsible they will be. Researchers also found that children who attend church on a regular basis are far less likely to be sexually active—so much for the presupposition that clinics must be morals-neutral. (Such a presupposition is impossible anyway because sex outside of marriage, and with multiple partners, cannot be a morally neutral issue. Either one chooses to have sex, or one does not; either way, he or she makes a moral decision.) Eighty-seven percent of children surveyed *did not want* comprehensive sexuality services in their schools, and only 28 percent thought clinics should be close to schools.

These are hardly the results Planned Parenthood had hoped for! In summary, Planned Parenthood's own survey found that:

• Almost 50 percent of eighteen-year-old girls were virgins.

• 20 percent who listed themselves as "sexually active" had only had sex once.

• Children with contraceptive information were more sexually active than those without it.

• Children who attend church are far less likely to be sexually active.

• 87 percent did *not* want comprehensive sexuality services in their schools.

• Only 28 percent thought clinics should even be *close* to schools.

Those are hardly the statistics we hear through the media. If one believes ABC, CBS, and NBC, sexual activity among teens is out of control and "government just has to do more!" Planned Parenthood did its best to conceal the results of the survey, and still managed to use the poll to its advantage by misrepresenting the results and then lamenting the "widespread ignorance" about contraception among teens. Planned Parenthood is selling contraceptive products, abortions, and a way of life that perpetuates a need for those things—and they certainly won't make $500 million a year telling the truth.

How Clinics Begin

In addition to Planned Parenthood, the Center for Population Options (CPO) is abetted on the local level by organizations like the Children's Defense Fund, the March of Dimes, the Urban League, and the YWCA.[16] Because the CPO is supported by groups claiming to have a deep concern for children, parents are often led to believe that a school-based clinic in their neighborhood will be a positive thing. Once a clinic is proposed in a given community, the CPO invites representatives from supporting organizations like those just mentioned to address residents. Speakers attempt to reassure opponents by emphasizing the need for health care and down-playing (or failing to mention altogether) the contraceptive (euphemistically called "family planning") services the clinic will offer. This is a deliberate misrepresentation, given the CPO's own admission that "by definition, *all of the clinics are involved in family planning*" (emphasis added).[17] Unfortunately for children, the CPO's strategy often throws dust in the eyes of parents who cannot see that the real purpose of SBCs is to distribute contraceptives and provide abortion counseling. Communities have also been fooled by proponents who convince taxpayers that private foundations will be footing the bill when that is only partially the case. Private foundations fund about one-third of the expenses. Taxpayers pay the remainder until the grant money runs out—usually after a year or two—then, individual communities get to pay for all of it.[18] The cost per child, per day of service, is about $73.88—higher than most private clinics.[19]

Johnson & Johnson, "The Baby Company"

School-based health clinics are sponsored in large part by the Robert Wood Johnson Foundation, an arm of Johnson & Johnson, the well-known health care corporation and maker of baby products. The second largest foundation in America, the Robert Wood Johnson Foundation has assets of more than $4 billion and believes that "Americans of all ages should have access to basic health care." They currently fund 41 percent of the SBCs on campuses across America.[20]

The Johnson Foundation admits that it would like to see health clinics on every public school campus. For now, they are concentrating on inner-city schools. It is significant to note that inner-city parents are often less educated and less involved in the schools than are their suburban counterparts. While it's true that the rate of teen pregnancy is higher in the inner city, it is also true that there are more single-parent households and less parental involvement on the campuses there. It's highly possible that SBCs are located in poor communities because parents are less likely to protest.

Johnson & Johnson makes hundreds of millions of dollars on baby products annually, so an increased number of babies can only help business grow. Equally notable is the fact that they also own Ortho Pharmaceutical Corporation, one of the largest manufacturers of birth control pills in the world. Either way, Johnson & Johnson stands to make hundreds of millions of dollars through school-based clinics every year. One can only imagine the enormous profit to Johnson & Johnson once the government begins to buy birth control pills—which account for 80 percent of the contraceptives dispersed or prescribed through school-based clinics—for all the new SBCs they are endorsing.

Questionable Success

Almost twenty years ago, St. Paul, Minnesota, reported that its SBC program was responsible for a 40 percent decrease in pregnancies and a 23 percent decline in births. Planned Parenthood continues to hold St. Paul up as an example of success, always forgetting to mention that the story is twenty years old. More significant is the fact that Planned Parenthood doesn't mention that the figures released by the St. Paul clinic were "based on the clinic's own records and/or the staff's knowledge," so data did not include all births or pregnancies. Further, clinic advocates did not include the number of pregnancies that ended in abortion (probably about 46 percent), nor did they mention that school enrollment declined by 25 percent. Therefore, researcher Marie Dietz concluded that the report that the birth rate dropped is "simply not supported by the data."[21]

Baltimore and Chicago also reported successes that did not hold up under scrutiny.[22] Therefore, it is safe to assume that there has never been a school-based clinic which has been successful in reducing the teen pregnancy rate.

A Look Inside Pandora's Box

Birth control pills account for 80 percent of the contraceptives dispersed or prescribed by school-based clinics. Heralded as the most effective form of birth control, teens are told that the Pill has only a 1 percent failure rate. However, several studies show the failure rate to be much higher.[23] As early as 1976, Planned Parenthood's own "Family Planning Perspective" reported that teens using the Pill regularly can expect a 5.8 percent pregnancy rate; since most teens use the Pill *irregularly*, a much higher failure rate must be anticipated.[24]

Inasmuch as girls on the Pill do not fear pregnancy, condoms are not used. Therefore, school-based clinics do nothing to prevent the spread of STDs or AIDS. According to the Centers for Disease Control, twelve million people contract some form of STD each year—a threefold increase since 1980, when the number of school-based clinics really began to increase. Further, the CDC reports that the rate among sixteen- to twenty-year-olds is three times higher than that of the general population.[25] Given those facts, the responsibility for the increase in teen herpes, gonorrhea, syphilis, and AIDS rests squarely on the shoulders of the morals-neutral adults who are teaching sex-ed and endorsing promiscuity by giving contraceptives to children. In addition, proponents must address the substantial amount of evidence that shows a link between early sexual activity and cervical cancer.[26]

Anyone who knows these facts and genuinely cares about children must admit that giving children more information about sex than they need to have, and then making contraceptives readily available to them, is like handing them a pistol and offering them "some fun" with a game of Russian roulette. Aside from the issue of morality, early sexual activity is harmful and dangerous. The parent's responsibility is not just to show children that sexual promiscuity is wrong. It is the job of every parent to let their children know that they are highly valued and deeply loved and that sexual abstinence is a wise decision for them to make because such a choice will protect the child from spiritual, physical, and emotional destruction. Parents dealing with a child who is already sexually active have a more difficult task, but, if a child senses unconditional love and the absence of negative judgment, it is often possible to reverse behavior.

Emotional Ramifications

SBCs do not address the serious issue of emotional trauma commensurate with early sexual activity. Many children may appear physiologically mature enough to engage in the act of intercourse during preteen and early teen years, but they are not emotionally mature enough to deal with the consequences that result from engaging in such an intimate act. In the Harris Poll cited earlier, 80 percent of the girls who admitted being sexually active felt they had been drawn into activity too soon. And, of those who admitted sexual activity, 84 percent said they wanted more information on how to say no "without hurting the other person's feelings."[27] That concern says a lot. Presumably, if one is mature enough to engage in something as adult as sexual activity, one should be mature enough to be able to refuse without worrying about hurting the other person's feelings!

When one thinks of the emotional trauma related to sex, one almost always pictures female victims. Though seldom noted, young men are also very emotionally affected by sexual relationships. No one likes rejection. Kathleen Sullivan, director of the highly successful abstinence-based program Project Respect, suggests that we "think in terms of this: almost every adult is . . . shattered by a broken physical union; how can we expect adolescents to go in and out of this highly charged physical state and not be affected?"[28] Abstinence programs stand alone in dealing realistically with the emotional aspect of sexual intimacy.

SBCs and sex-ed courses that focus on the "right" and acceptability of gratifying selfish, immediate needs but ignore the greater need for emotional and spiritual growth do a tremendous amount of harm to the development of teens. If proponents of SBCs and comprehensive sex-ed courses really care about the welfare of children, shouldn't the child's emotional well-being be, at least, as much of a consideration as their physical pleasure?

The fact that school-based clinics promote promiscuity is evidenced by the fact that 65 percent of children using them were not sexually active prior to clinic participation.[29] With results like that, if not for the fact that family planning clinics made $150 million for Planned Parenthood last year, even *they* could not justify keeping them open. Teen pregnancy is not the problem; it is only a symptom of the problem of sexual promiscuity, and it is impossible for school-based clinics to solve the very problem they exacerbate, by virtue of their presence.

Clinic proponents believe it's better to give out contraceptives than to teach children the virtues of chastity and self-control. In their efforts to keep kids "safe," well-meaning but misled individuals forget that character development is equally as important as physical development. Children want and need guidance from adults who care about their souls, as well as their bodies. We must all question the degree of caring and real commitment of those who would rather hand a child a condom and send him on his way than spend an hour helping him to identify the difference between selfish gratification and a meaningful relationship based on mutual self-respect and purity. SBCs lack any interest in a child's moral development.

Drug Rehab

Social services are "offered to individual schools, based upon the school's specific need." At the present time, inner-city schools are most likely to have school-based clinics because the incidents of teen pregnancy, violent crime, and drug addiction are more prevalent there. More than one-third of all SBCs serve patients other than students enrolled in the school where the clinic is located.[30] Because drug intervention programs are also offered in high-risk areas, there is a potential danger to students in that they may be exposed to drug addicts going to those facilities for counseling or treatment. The same danger exists when sex offenders attend counseling sessions at clinics located in public schools.

Condoms R Us

Based on the proven false assumption that most teens are going to have sex, the National Research Council issued a report in which they encouraged widespread distribution of contraceptives through school-based clinics.[31] One of those clinics displays a poster that claims (completely erroneously), "Use condoms, there's living proof they stop AIDS."

Without exception, studies prove that condoms do not provide adequate protection from STDs or AIDS.[32] Chlamydia, the fastest growing STD, begins as a painless pimple or blister on the penis or vagina. About two to twelve weeks later, the lymph nodes in the groin become painfully enlarged, mat together, redden, and drain pus. Later, ugly ulcers appear on the genitals. Dr. William R. Archer, former deputy secretary of Health and Human Services, claims that chlamydia is so infectious, there is a 50 percent chance of transmitting it with one encounter.[33] Studies show that, after "a period of time" in a sexual relationship, condoms offer no protection at all from this terrible disease. Archer further claims that, though condoms are "touted as the great cure-all for AIDS and pregnancy," they are *not*.

One out of three sexually active teenagers will acquire an STD before graduating from high school. And, in most cases, a condom would have done little to stop it.[34]

Dr. Joe McIlhaney, Jr. agrees: "The philosophy that directs teens to 'be careful' or 'to play it safe with condoms' has not protected them. It has only enticed them into the quagmire of venereal warts, genital cancer and precancer, herpes for life, infertility, and AIDS."[35]

The truth about the government's lack of a responsible AIDS policy is becoming widely known. The clamor from the conservative community is growing louder and demanding action. Feeling the heat, the Centers for Disease Control (CDC) released a report in August of 1993, in which they claimed that condoms *were* effective in preventing HIV infection. Then, they cited two studies as "proof" of their claim—both of which proved them absolutely wrong!

The CDC claimed that latex condoms "substantially reduce the risk for HIV transmission," citing a study done by Dr. Susan Weller, who, in her conclusions, said the exact opposite! Weller analyzed data from eleven different studies, concluding that "since contraceptive research indicates condoms are about 90 percent effective in preventing pregnancy, many people, even physicians, assume condoms prevent HIV transmission with the same degree of effectiveness. However, HIV transmission studies do not show this to be true."[36]

The second study cited revealed that "anatomic differences make STDs [and, subsequently, AIDS] more easily transferable to . . . women." In addition, that study found the failure rate of condoms in preventing pregnancy to be "at least 12%." Other studies show the failure rate to be as high as 18 percent when condoms are used by teen-agers, who may not know how to use them properly. This means that roughly one in five girls who depends upon a condom will end up pregnant,[37] and many more than that will end up with a sexually transmitted disease or AIDS.

As you will see in the text following, the failure rate for HIV transmission through a latex condom is much higher than it is for sperm. However, it is highly unlikely that a "morally neutral" nurse practitioner would take the time to warn a child of that fact. Indeed, how could any conscionable person hand a child a condom and say, "Here. And . . . oh, by the way, you might get AIDS and die." Anyone with a conscience would never give a child a condom in the first place, knowing that it is highly probable that that child could contract AIDS. Anyone—child or adult—who thinks that a condom will protect them from AIDS should think again.

The Legacy of C. Everett Koop

Former surgeon general, C. Everett Koop, assumed responsibility for the HIV infection of tens of thousands of people when he issued a statement saying, "If your partner has a positive blood test showing that he/she has been infected with the AIDS virus . . . a rubber (condom) should always be used." The implication is: there is no danger of HIV infection if condoms are used. One would expect that "if the surgeon general says it, it's got to be true," but research proves Koop's statement 100 percent wrong and totally irresponsible. Now, "Condom Queen" Joycelyn Elders—a title she affectionately gave herself— continues Koop's irresponsible legacy by tossing condoms like confetti at school children, knowing better than most that condom distribution *increases* the rate of teen sexual activity.

Elders is also an advocate of Norplant, which she'd like to make available through *all* school-based clinics. Norplant, a five-year contraceptive implant, is inserted in the arm so near the surface of the skin that anyone touching the arm can feel it. Besides the fact that Norplant cannot prevent STDs or AIDS, the appearance of it under the skin alerts young men that the recipient is sexually active.

With Bill Clinton comfortably in the Arkansas governor's mansion and Elders leading the charge to distribute condoms, teen pregnancy in the state of Arkansas increased by 15 percent! Also during that time, reported cases of syphilis increased by 130 percent—a strong indicator of what is to come now that Bill and Hillary have brought their brand of "family values" into the White House. The fact is no one in government is acknowledging the truth about condoms—least of all the surgeon general of the United States! Overwhelming evidence by independent researchers proves beyond any doubt that the state is wrong in its liberal policy regarding contraceptive distribution.

Our government spends billions of dollars to fan the hysteria flame about "global warming," yet there is absolutely no empirical evidence to prove that global warming exists. By contrast, government has never allocated funds to research the effectiveness of condoms before giving them to our children—often behind our backs. Independent agencies and researchers, obviously much more concerned about the public welfare than politicians are, have conducted studies, and, in addition to those already cited, this is what some of them found:

The Consumer's Union reported a significant failure rate in condoms, due to leakage and deterioration. Recently, Dr. David Hager (formerly of the CDC) reported that latex condoms often have small cracks in them, generally about five microns in size. Though such a small defect is almost invisible to the naked eye, the AIDS virus measures only 0.1 of a micron in size, making it easy for the virus to escape through the condom crack into the body.[38] The failure rate of condoms, when relied upon to prevent pregnancy, varies according to the study one reads, but all researchers—even condom manufacturers—agree that condoms fail. On average, about thirteen of every one hundred women will become pregnant while using condoms for protection—even though a woman is fertile only a few days each month.[39] Now, contrast that reality with the fact that HIV is alive 365 days per year and is three hundred to four hundred times *smaller* than a sperm cell. Thus, researchers estimate the failure rate of condoms when used as protection from HIV to be as high as *50 percent.*

While serving as health director for the state of Arkansas, Joycelyn Elders distributed defective condoms to thousands of school children. No one knows how many of those children became pregnant as a result of her despicable action or, worse, how many of those children contracted HIV and will subsequently die, after infecting others. Elders has made condom distribution a priority since Bill Clinton (regrettably) appointed her surgeon general of the United States. Someone once said of Elders, "To understand her, you have to start with the cotton." I agree with that, but the cotton is not in the fields of Arkansas as the speaker indicated; it's between Joycelyn's ears, where her brain ought to be, and it directs her heart, which has been hardened by a godless, liberal ideology that is adding to the destruction of the moral fiber of this nation's youth. Aside from the fact that she is grossly ill-equipped for the job of surgeon general, Elders' philosophy is repugnant. As a tax-paying citizen forced to pay for those condoms, I'd like to know: "Who is liable if a child becomes infected or impregnated while using a defective condom given to him or her by the U.S. government without parental knowledge or consent?" Would Elders be liable? Or the school district? Or the condom manufacturer? Certainly, if a minor child is involved, *someone* is responsible.

In an interview in *The Advocate*, Elders claims that homosexual "sex is wonderful . . . and a healthy part of our being." No one but Elders knows how she knows that, if she really believes it, or if she's just made the announcement in the interest of political correctness. What we do know is that it's an incredibly irresponsible statement for any public health official to make in lieu of all the evidence to the contrary! In making such a statement, Elders, given her position as surgeon general, must assume much of the blame for the continued spread of AIDS.

Elders claims to love homosexuals, while ignoring numerous studies proving that the risk of HIV infection while using a condom is much higher for homosexuals than it is for heterosexuals. The membrane in condoms has proven insufficient to hold up during anal sex. In the first controlled study of condom use exclusively by homosexuals, condoms failed 26 percent of the time.[40] In another study, when prostitutes used condoms strictly in conjunction with anal sex, they failed as much as 50 percent of the time.[41] Still, Elders and other homosexual activists continue to promote the use of condoms in the homosexual community, falsely promising that those who use them will be safe from AIDS.

In a study of families where one or more members was HIV positive, Dr. Margaret Fischl of the University of Miami revealed that 17 percent of infected males transmitted HIV to their mates while using a condom. Eighty-two percent infected their mates because they were not using condoms, but, of those abstaining from sex, not a single case of transmission was reported. To conclude that condom use equals safe sex is to conclude that a bullet through the heart might make you "a little bit dead." When it comes to the AIDS virus, there is no such thing as safe sex, and *that's* what our children should be taught.

What our children are learning in public schools today is sex outside the context of traditional biblical morality—sex that will ultimately kill them by the hundreds of thousands—unless parents take a firm stand and demand that schools begin to teach abstinence and morality and tell the truth about condom use and the spread of HIV. Instead of a doctrine of immorality without consequences, children must be taught the value of morality and abstinence—the only certain deterrents to early parenthood and sexually transmitted diseases. Equally important, children who choose to remain abstinent must be highly commended.

The National Education Association consistently resists all efforts to teach morality in the classroom. The concept of morality dictates boundaries and demands definitions of "right" and "wrong"—moral absolutes which the NEA denies. In their quest to promote humanist values, the NEA is poisoning our children with filth and lying to them about AIDS. It cannot be said enough that people like Bill and Hillary Clinton, Joycelyn Elders, and Planned Parenthood proponents—while perhaps well-meaning—do not understand that the biggest problem we have is that children are being taught that *anything* is permissible. The humanist, values-neutral philosophy has led children to believe that there is something wrong with saying that something is wrong! Liberal educators and godless politicians have taken advantage of the fact that many parents are uninformed and underinvolved, and they have stepped in to train our children for us.

There has never been a survey done that showed public support for school-based health clinics, yet the number of clinics is rapidly increasing. Parents and students absolutely and overwhelmingly object to the present clinics, yet few communities are willing to spend the time or effort required to fight the issue. The same is true of comprehensive sex-ed; the curriculum is humiliating and embarrassing to most students, and most do not agree with its prohomosexual content or its endorsement of promiscuity. The conservative community cannot continue to cry "foul" while doing nothing. For years, the facts have been concealed. Now, the facts are laid bare, and the tragic consequences of liberal ideology are well known and admirably documented. Armed with the *truth*, we must fight back!

If there is already a SBC in your neighborhood, do some research. If clinic practices are objectionable to the majority, work to shut the clinic down or, at least, to halt the distribution of contraceptives from the clinic. In communities where SBCs do not yet exist, call your school superintendent and ask whether there are plans pending to open one. If plans exist, find out who's involved, and seek profamily representation immediately. Quote statistics on the increased rate of sexual promiscuity, pregnancy, and abortions resulting from the presence of SBCs. Focus on the government's own HHS study. Though liberals often fail to acknowledge the truth in spite of the facts, numbers don't lie!

According to Kathleen Sullivan, we can all write Congress and insist that Title X money be split three ways: A third for abstinence programs, a third for adoption, and "let them keep the other third [for liberal sex-ed programs]."[42] Then, let's insist on an evaluation of the results! Likewise, parents opposed to the idea of condom distribution in schools can write their congressmen and congresswomen and demand that government stop encouraging promiscuity and absence itself from dictating immorality.

Any parent with knowledge of a child who has gotten pregnant or contracted a sexually transmitted disease or AIDS as a result of using a government-distributed condom given to a minor without parental consent, should seek legal counsel to determine liability.

Given the high increase in teen promiscuity and the subsequent rise in the spread of sexually transmitted diseases, teen pregnancy, and AIDS, it is impossible to consider the implications of school-based clinics, apart from the significant moral and philosophical issues involved. Solutions to the problems we face as a society will not be found in school-based health clinics; they will be found in churches.

Endnotes

1. Peter LaBarbera, "Teens Go for Abstinence," *Family Voice* (March 1993): 4.

2. Stan E. Weed and Joseph A Olsen, "Policy and Program Considerations for Teenage Pregnancy Prevention: A Summary for Policymakers," *Family Perspective*, vol. 22, no. 3 (1986): 239.

3. D. Kirby, "Sexuality Education: A More Realistic View of Its Effects," *Journal of School Health*, vol. 55: 421-424.

4. Marian Wallace, "Sex Education: Failing to Make the Grade," *Family Voice* (September 1993): 4.

5. Ibid.

6. Ibid., 241.

7. Dean Gardner and Mark Beuchler, "School Based Health Clinics," Policy Memo Series No. 4 (January 1989), from the Consortium on Educational Policy Studies (School of Education, Indiana University), 4.

8. Ibid., 5.

9. Gardner & Beuchler, "School Based Health," 22.

10. "School Based Clinics Falsely Claim to Be the Answer to Teen Pregnancy" (Concerned Women for America [January 1990]): 6.

11. George Grant and Mark A. Horne, *Legislating Immorality* (Chicago: Moody Press, 1993), 78.

12. "New Study: Government-funded Birth Control, Sex Ed Leads to Increase in Teenage Pregnancies," *Education Reporter*, no. 7 (August 1986).

13. Ibid.

14. Ibid.

15. Gardner & Beuchler, "School Based Health," 18.

16. Dinah Richard, Ph.D., *Has Sex Education Failed Our Teenagers? A Research Report* (Pomona, CA: Focus on the Family Publishing, 1990), 13.

17. Faye Wattleton, *The Humanist* (July/August 1986): 7.

18. "School Based Clinics," 6.

19. Richard, *Has Sex Education Failed?*, 14.

20. Gardner and Beuchler, "School Based Health," 8.

21. Richard, *Has Sex Education Failed?*, 15.

22. Ibid.

23. Ibid., 23.

24. Ibid.

25. Ibid., 24.

26. S.L. Barron, "Sexual Activity in Girls Under 16 Years of Age," *British Journal of Obstetrics and Gynecology*, vol. 93 (1986): 787. Cited by D. Richard, *Has Sex Education Failed?* 24.

27. M. Howard and J.B. McCabe, "Helping Teenagers Postpone Sexual Involvement," *Family Planning Perspectives*, vol. 22, no. 1, (January/February 1990): 21-26.

28. "Abstinence: The One Choice That Works!" *Family Voice* (March 1993): 11.

29. Tom Phillips, "Series Called 'Propaganda,' " *Milwaukee Journal* (17 February 1990): editorial page.

30. S.R. Lovick and R.F. Stern, "The School-Based Clinic: 1988 Update" (Washington, D.C.: Center for Population Options).

31. Debra Viadero, "Wide Distribution of Contraceptives Advocated," *Education Week* (17 December 1896): 1.

32. S. Samuels, "Chlamydia: Epidemic Among America's Young," *Medical Aspects of Human Sexuality* (December 1989): 16-24.

33. Ibid.

34. Dr. Glen C, Griffin, "Condoms and Contraceptives in Junior High and High School Clinics: What Do You Think?" *Postgraduate Medicine*, vol. 93, no. 5 (April 1993): 1-6.

35. Ibid., 5.

36. UTMB News, University of Texas Medical Branch at Galveston, 7 June 1993, as quoted by Glenn T. Stanton, M.A., in his report "Condom Efficacy and Social Policy," the focus on the family physicians advisory council, March 1994, 2.

37. W.R. Grady, M.D. Hayward and J. Yagi, "Contraceptive Failure in the United States: Estimates from the 1982 National Survey of Family Growth," *Family Planning Perspective*, vol. 18, no. 5 (1986): 200-209.

38. Dr. Susan Weller, University of Texas Medical School, "A Meta-analysis of Condom Effectiveness in Reducing Sexually Transmitted HIV," *Social Science & Medicine* (1993) as cited in *Family Research Report* (July-August 1993).

39. Ibid.

40. The report, which appeared in the *British Medical Jour-*

nal, was referred to in a research paper and not adequately footnoted.

41. Reported in *Lancet* (21 December 1985), cited by Dr. Paul Cameron, *Exposing the AIDS Scandal* (Lafayette, LA: Huntington House Books, 1993), 86.

42. LaBarbera "Abstinence": 9.

7

The U.N. Convention on the Rights of the Child

All authority on heaven and on earth has been given to me.

—Matthew 28:18

In a free country, there can be no autonomy of the individual. All elements of society–the individual, the group, and the sovereign power of the state–participate in a dance of checks and balances, with each bowing to the necessary authority of the other, and all submissive to the Divine Power which is over all.
—James P. Lucier, Ph.D.
(former minority staff director,
U.S. Senate Foreign
Relations Committee)

In the second chapter of Genesis, it is clear that God ordained the family. Throughout the Bible, He defines the role and obligations of parents and makes it clear that all are responsible to Him for "training up" children in the way they should go. Through His Word, God establishes the need for parental authority and discipline over the children He gives us[1] and clearly defines every parent's responsibility to teach his own children and raise them according to biblical principles (Deut. 4:9-10). In defiant opposition to God's law, the U.N. Convention on the Rights of the Child (CRC) ordains the state, "Head of Each House."

Like the United Nations organization itself, this treaty has no place for God or His precepts and deems children and parents minions of government. The CRC allows a godless international organization—the United Nations— to force its obtrusive philosophy for a humanist, one-world government on the free citizens of America.

Understanding the Convention

A "Convention" is an international agreement that has the force of a treaty and usually relates to a single topic—in this case, the topic (presumably) is children's rights. Throughout history, treaties have been written between independent governments for the purpose of settling disputes, ending wars, and regulating relations. The U.N. Convention on the Rights of the Child is different from traditional treaties in that it was initiated for the sole purpose of forcing the U.N.'s idea of how children should be raised upon the rest of the world. Through this treaty, the U.N. wants to give all children, worldwide, complete autonomy from parental authority.

An in-depth study of the history of the U.N. would be most appropriate for any readers who are uninformed regarding that organization's primary agenda and motive. For the purpose of analyzing this one treaty, readers must understand that the U.N. was created in an effort to remake the social structure for the purpose of advancing the globalist (one-world government) philosophy of its founders. Given that agenda, if the U.N. can control the children of America through this treaty, it can control the future destiny of the United States. If the United States Senate ratifies the U.N. Convention on the Rights of the Child, it will become the international and domestic obligation of every American parent to raise their children according to U.N. dictates.

If signed by the president, the Senate will receive the treaty. Because the Senate is designed to be a body representative of the people, it is presumed that the treaty will be debated. Those opposed to ratification are gravely concerned because the treaty has not yet been debated, but it has widespread support in the Senate already. It is doubtful whether those supporting the treaty have read the document in its entirety. Public servants committed to the protection of the U.S. Constitution and the rights of individual families could never in good conscience sign the U.N. treaty.

The United States functions on the principle of common law theory, for the common good. Our Founding Fathers believed that the rights of individuals were established by one Creator, and our Constitution is predicated upon that belief. By contrast, the founders of the United Nations denied the existence of God and believed that all men must be subject to government. According to the Family Research Council, "the UN Convention on the Rights of the Child is a product of civil law [as opposed to common law] thinking; and, as such, it will always remain a hostile alien to the common law [of the United States]."[2]

Common law uses cases already tried in court as examples. It is based on the prior decisions of judges and the application of precedents used to guarantee justice. Under common law, United States judges do not have the right to depart from previous precedents, nor do they have a right to create new ones. The American system of common law is not based upon any definition of individual rights and cannot be determined apart from the knowledge of specific facts in any given case. The U.N. treaty, however, assumes to determine the best interests of all children before any case has been heard. Under the law of this treaty, the child will prevail no matter what.

Hidden underneath the liberal double-speak which declares the treaty "a landmark in international efforts to strengthen justice, peace, and freedom in the world through the promotion and protection of human rights"[3] lies insidious government subterfuge. In reading the documents given to members of the U.N. when the treaty was first introduced, there is little wonder that the convention was unanimously adopted. The U.N.'s World Declaration on the Survival, Protection and Development of Children is a heart-rending analysis of the plight of children throughout the world. It declares the dilemma of children described as "curious, active and full of hope." It implores readers to take notice of the need for those "innocent, vulnerable children to be protected," and it challenges them to consider *all* children who are constantly "exposed to dangers" and forced to "suffer immensely as casualties of war and violence . . . , victims of discrimination . . . and aggression," who are "forced to abandon their homes."

The literature issued to sell the treaty to U.N. delegates implores them to consider the millions of children "suffering from the scourges of poverty . . . hunger and homelessness, epidemics and illiteracy, and degradation of the environment." The document continued for five pages until, I'm sure, there was probably not a dry eye in the assembly. Having read it myself, I understand that well-meaning delegates signed it, thinking that doing so would help children who are suffering. However, those who signed the treaty certainly did so based on the document's emotional appeal and not on the contents of the treaty itself.

Certainly, no one denies that terrible circumstances *do* exist for far too many children. No one with a beating heart can pick up a daily paper and not be emotionally torn by the predicament of millions of children in America and abroad. The worldwide presence of the American Red Cross, Christian missionaries, and Peace Corp volunteers stands as honorable testimony of the entire world's concern and commitment to children everywhere. But, those problems noted in the U.N.'s literature have absolutely nothing to do with this treaty, nor does the treaty offer a single solution to any of those problems.

In its fact sheet on the treaty, the U.N. states that, in the last thirty years, "many perceptions [about children's rights] have changed and new ideas have emerged." No one disputes that fact, but whose ideas are they, and how will those ideas affect the American family? Currently, the traditional American family lies wounded and bleeding on the battlefield of the cultural war; if this treaty is ratified, it will be like a deadly bayonet thrust through the heart. Never before has any pending legislation posed such an ominous threat to the survival of the traditional American family.

Accompanying the World Declaration document was an annex titled "Plan of Action for Implementing the World Declaration." Like the declaration itself, it's pure propaganda and avoids altogether explaining the real purpose of the treaty, which is to make your child—and every child born in America—a ward of the state.

The Treaty Defined

The U.N. reports that, following adoption by the General Assembly, the CRC was opened for signature in January 1990. Immediately, sixty-one countries signed the document—a record response, according to the United Nations. (Signature indicates that the nations signing will ratify the treaty, given the approval of the necessary authorities in those countries.) Once ratified, signatory nations must review their national laws to make sure they comply with those in the treaty. In addition, each nation must declare itself bound to observe the treaty's provisions and "becomes answerable to the international community."[4]

For the most part, the public has remained perilously uninformed about the U.N. convention because it's mov-

ing at break-neck speed through all channels. According
to the U.N., that speed indicates "world-wide interest and
support" for the convention. In reality, it indicates that
subversive forces are doing their job well, and well behind the backs of the American people. Indeed, the draft-
ers of this legislation stand in violation of their own Article 42, which promises to make "the principles and provisions of the Convention widely known . . . to adults and
children alike."

This treaty, which claims to protect the rights of children, actually terminates the rights of parents and gives
government unrestrained authority over every American
child. Even the ACLU—always to the extreme Left on
issues involving the traditional family—has questions about
the possible ramifications of some of the treaty's provisions. When describing the impact that children's rights
legislation could have on the lives of children, the ACLU's
Marcia Lowry asks, "Is it helpful for children to have a
right of education against a government that is denying
them that right? I think undeniably, yes. Is it helpful for
a child to have rights that a court will recognize against a
parent in an intact family? Probably not."[5]

If ratified, government bureaucrats—not parents—will
have the right to determine "the best interest of the child."
This treaty is not at all about protecting children's rights;
it's about power—and who will exercise that power over
our children. Indeed, if the real intent here were to protect children from abuse, the legislation would be super-
fluous anyway; the United States already has common
and statutory laws designed exclusively to prosecute child
abusers. While parts of the treaty will, indeed, help to
protect children, for the most part, the "child protection"
language is just an enticement to lure support for the
treaty.

If ratified, the CRC will subvert the family by giving
children autonomous "rights" to rebel against their parents—rights that will make it possible for them to sue

their parents in court—for everything from spanking them (a violation of Article 19!) to making them attend church on Sundays—and they could probably win. According to public-service attorney, Gabe Kaimowitz, "Theoretically, I can win anything for a child in court where an adult has a comparable right." (And he has that assurance without ratification of this treaty!)[6]

Civil court proceedings will be brought against those who violate the treaty. In opposition to constitutional law, civil law theory determines justice by relying on abstract principles linked to current philosophies. It's significant to note that civil court proceedings differ greatly from the common law proceedings that all Americans understand. In a court of civil law, the judge (not a grand jury) first examines the evidence before the trial and then brings action against the defendant. If the judge determines that the defendant is guilty, the defendant must prove himself innocent. If a jury is called at all, it will not be a jury of the defendant's peers; it will be a mixed jury of laymen and judicial officials appointed by the state, and they need not be unanimous in their verdict.[7]

In a civil law proceeding, written arguments are substituted for oral presentations, and it is the judge who asks questions, discovers evidence, and advances the legal principles. A judge who sets a defendant free, based on the precedent set in a previous case, would be seen as lacking judicial temperament.[8] When compared to U.S. constitutional law, the U.N.'s perception of liberty must be seen as profoundly and radically different.

The U.N. treaty strips biological parents of the right to raise their own children and transfers that right to the state, making government the absolute guardian. Until now, American citizens have come to view the raising of our children in the privacy of our own homes as sacrosanct and safe from state intervention. If this treaty becomes law, the state will have the right to barge in without knocking.

What Rights?

Among other things, the CRC grants children autonomous rights to privacy, public health education, free primary education, government subsidized and run child care-services, freedom of association, and freedom of expression. As one might expect, the "rights" granted imply far more than they appear to on the surface. In his Special Report on the Convention, Douglas Phillips notes the significance of the fact that four of God's Ten Commandments protect the integrity of the family by denying the very forms of "expression" enshrined in the U.N. treaty.

Article 2: RIGHT TO FREEDOM FROM DISCRIMINATION: At face value, no one would argue. But, when closely examined, one sees that the child's interest is not at heart, as much as the treaty is concerned with impinging on parental rights. This article guarantees the child certain rights, irrespective of the parent's views, and mandates state intervention on behalf of the child if the parent objects. For example, under this treaty, a child cannot be discriminated against on the basis of "race, color, sex, language, religion, political or other opinion." Keeping in mind that the treaty grants these rights to "all children under the age of 18," imagine that your fourteen-year-old announces that he no longer believes in God. He proclaims himself an atheist and tells you he's not going to church on Sunday and that if you make him go, he'll sue you for discrimination because you're denying him the right to choose his own religion. Lest you think your child would never do that, be warned that some public schools are currently coaching students on how to do it!

Article 3: THE RIGHT TO DETERMINE BEST INTEREST: The treaty declares that "in all actions concerning children," the government is empowered to regulate families, based on their subjective determination of the best interest of the child. "States Parties," Article 3 says, "shall take all appropriate legislative and administrative measures" on behalf of the child. This article gives complete authority to government and divests parents of their right to determine what is best for their own children.

"Best interest of the child" is a legal principle. In the case of divorce, courts use the principle to determine what arrangements to make after the divorce is granted and after the court has ruled that there has been a failure in the family. Recently, in many cases where children are home-schooled, the state has made efforts to use the "best interest" standard as a rule of law when it is not. If asserted as law, the rule allows the court to substitute its own view for that of the parent's. Parents prevail in most cases, but not in all.

If the U.N. treaty is ratified, state agents will have a legal right to make subjective judgments about what is best for a child—before the court has determined that there is a problem in the home to begin with.[9] Under this law, the state could determine that it's "best" for a minor child to have an abortion or—the other extreme—for a child to be sterilized. (Governments have been known to make such determinations regarding retarded individuals.) If your child is on life support, the government may legally determine whether it's in his "best interest" to live. (If national health care becomes a reality, the state could have less interest in keeping your child alive, as the state will be picking up the tab.) Quite simply, best interest of the child is determined by U.N. dictates, *not* by the child's family.

Article 5: THE STATE SHALL RESPECT THE RIGHTS OF PARENTS: Parental rights as granted by the U.N. convention are purely inane. When read and interpreted in its complete context, the U.N. treaty mandates that parents have legal rights only to the extent that they do not interfere with or oppose the rights already granted to children under the treaty. In other words, if children and parents disagree, the child always prevails.

Article 6: THE INHERENT RIGHT TO LIFE: The treaty claims that "every child has the inherent right to life," but, again, the statement contradicts the actions: The majority of signatory nations permit and actively encourage abortions. Further, the "right to privacy" granted children under Article 16 assures that any child who wants an abortion can get one without parental knowledge or consent. Article 16 would presumably create an across-the-board right to abortion by virtue of the fact that it says, "No child shall be subjected to arbitrary or unlawful interference with his or her privacy." Article 24 (f) establishes the right to "family planning education services." Most certainly, those "services" will include school-based health clinics where your child can get contraceptives or directions to an abortuary.

Article 9: THE RIGHT TO BE SEPARATED FROM PARENTS: Parents will no longer have the right to deny a child anything based upon their own convictions or religious beliefs. Should they attempt to, the state may remove the child from his parents if "competent authorities . . . determine . . . that such separation is necessary."

Article 13: THE RIGHT TO FREEDOM OF EXPRESSION: Under Article 13 of the convention, children are granted the right to "freedom of expression." There is no provision for parental guidance within the confines of this article; every child is granted absolute freedom of expression from the day he or she is born. A child is free to use any language he deems necessary in order to "express" himself. A parent may not tell a child what to watch on television, what movies he may not see, or what books and magazines he cannot read. Parents who restrict a child's right to "seek, receive and impart information and ideas of all kinds, regardless of frontiers, either orally, in writing or in print, in the form of art, or through *any other media of the child's choice*" (emphasis added) can be subject to prosecution for denying the child his "right of unlimited expression."

Article 14: THE RIGHT TO FREEDOM OF THOUGHT, CONSCIENCE AND RELIGION: Article 14 gives children the right to reject religious training imposed by their parents and overrides parental objections to their participation in occult or alternative religions.

Article 15: THE RIGHT TO FREEDOM OF ASSOCIATION AND ASSEMBLY: This could mean a sixteen-year-old girl's "right" to keep company with a man twenty years older or a teenage boy's "right" to associate with drug dealers or gang members. If your child wants to attend a heavy-metal rock concert where you know drugs and a potential for danger exist, you have no right to stop him. Legally, "freedom of association" could mean sexual involvement with an adult or minor children gathering in topless bars. It's a given that, eventually, there will be no more legal drinking or age-of-consent laws because, when considered in its entirety, it could be argued that this treaty gives children a legal right to do whatever they please. Restricting them from going to bars or having sex would violate their rights to free association and assembly.

Article 16: THE RIGHT TO PRIVACY: Legally, the "right to privacy" could be interpreted to mean the right of a minor child to have an abortion or receive birth control without informing her parents. It would also remove parental protections from children who could be exposed to experimental drugs or surgeries used by the state, even though one of the treaty's primary framers admits that medical experimentation on children is "an all-too-frequent reality."[10] It's a matter of record that experimental contraceptive methods are currently being used in Third World countries. With the destiny of RU486 still undetermined, we cannot assume that any of our daughters will be safe from experimentation with that drug. Given the growing number of school-based health clinics and the government's zeal for handing out contraceptives and advice, it is not unlikely that, if legalized, RU486 could be handed out in school-based health clinics right along with the condoms and the birth control pills. Another area of concern is the common use of medication to quiet "hyperactive" children or those diagnosed with Attention Deficit Disorder. Under this treaty, government may determine whether or not your child is hyperactive and whether or not the use of a drug is "in his best interest."

The absolute "right to privacy" granted in this article means that if your minor child wants to engage in sexual activity in the privacy of his or her own bedroom, parents have no right under the law to interfere. In fact, if you do, you could be legally charged with a crime! The article insists that no one (meaning the parent) has a right to "arbitrarily interfere" with a child's privacy. Likewise, if your teen-ager's door is closed and you smell marijuana fumes wafting thru the air, you do not have a right to enter the room and confront him. Further, if the student who sold your child the marijuana is suspected of bringing a gun to school, the administration will not have the right to search his locker. When addressing the issue of violence in the schools, a New York City teacher said, "A search happens very seldom today, because we are so conscious of the youngsters' rights." But, what about the rights of the students who must attend school *with the child who has the gun?*

Article 27: THE RIGHT TO A CERTAIN STANDARD OF LIVING: This article requires parents to implement "a standard of living adequate for the child's physical, mental, spiritual, moral and social development." But the treaty does not define what any of those decrees actually mean. So, what happens when a child feels that a $150 pair of sneakers is imperative for his "social development," but you, as a parent, can't afford them? What if your daughter, who's already angry with you, has her heart set on a car you can't afford? Could she haul you into court and successfully convince the judge that a new car is necessary for her social development and well-being? Could she argue that the car she has is six years old and could pose a threat to her safety—even though you know it doesn't? Such possibilities are not unrealistic when considering the vast implications of this treaty, the limitless rights it grants to children, and the liberalism so pervasive in courtrooms today.

Given the proper circumstances, any parent, regardless of how "good" the parent-child relationship is, could be subject to prosecution. At some point, every child gets angry enough at his parents to do something drastic. Under this treaty, once a child reports his parents—no matter how frivolous or unfounded the charges—and the government becomes involved, there is no turning back; the child who has been given so many "irrevocable rights" by government does *not* have the right *not to prosecute* his own parents!

Most children under the age of eighteen are not mature enough to always think rationally and, thus, make determinations that are in their own best interest—if they were, God would have designed them to be born as adults! There's a reason children are born small and then grow up: As they are loved, nurtured, and cared for by their parents, their physical bodies grow. As their bodies are growing, parents who love them teach them to walk and talk and interact with others. Parents who have a personal, vested interest in the welfare of their children spend time with them. They care about what's happening in their child's life each day, and they offer guidance and counsel in making decisions. Parents, *not government agents*, tuck their children in bed and read them stories. Parents who love their children make sacrifices. They sit next to the child's bed when he's sick, and they give up a much desired night out alone, so they can afford to take the kids to the zoo on Saturday. And, responsible parents discipline their children with love when they misbehave. I do not believe Bill Clinton when he says government "feels our pain." Nor do I agree with Hillary, who has made (on more than one occasion) the radical statement that a child's presence within the family unit "can be equated to slavery." Government is not personal and feels no one's pain. Parents care about their children. Government, as manifested in the U.N. treaty, cares only about controlling them.

The U.N. Treaty and Your Child's Education

It is imperative to know that the U.N.'s concept of education is entirely statist and that its educational charter is devoted to humanist values and the advance of globalism. According to Article 29, it is the goal of the state to direct the education of all whom it governs toward a globalist philosophy, as "enshrined in the charter of the United Nations." They plan to prepare each child to be a "responsible citizen" by having "the spirit of understanding, peace, toleration, equity of sexes, and friendship [for] all peoples, ethnic, national, and religious groups of indigenous origin." Translated: Ethical pluralism, one-world government, and the complete and utter dissolution of the Republic of the United States of America as it was founded and as we know it.

Article 28: THE RIGHT TO FREE EDUCATION: This article guarantees every child the right to education and maintains that the state's duty is to ensure that every child gets it "free" of charge. The treaty claims that parents have no right to expect education to conform to their value system and encourages alternate forms of secondary education. Given the Goals 2000 mandate, that could mean almost anything. Supposedly, the state wants our children to have "different experiences," so they can determine on their own what they want to believe. Thus, government gave us Outcome Based Education, which, instead of encouraging independent thought, brainwashes students into accepting the liberal humanistic philosophies of an organization with ambitions toward a socialist one-world government. We have sex-ed classes that encourage children to view sexual perversity and promiscuity as normal and social studies courses that blatantly teach children to rebel against authority. History classes now invite students to rewrite the past until it makes them feel good, and science classrooms have become laboratories for experimentation in the paranormal. Using the state's idea of "different forms" of education, it's commonplace for world religion and philosophy to be discussed at length in the public schools, while discussions of Christianity, or any mention of the God of the Bible, is almost nonexistent.

Section 1 (e) of Article 28 gives government the right to "take measures to encourage regular attendance at schools," but the treaty doesn't specify what those measures are or how they will be taken. Given the state's contempt for home-schoolers, it can be assumed that government will interpret the phrase "regular attendance *at schools*" to mean that literally. Apart from the treaty, government recently tried to sneak legislation through Congress that would have required that home-school teachers (parents) be certified in every subject they taught. Had it not been for the astute action of the Home School Legal Defense Fund, H.R. 6 would have all but obliterated home-schools in America.

DISCIPLINE CONSISTENT WITH HUMAN DIGNITY: Section 2 of Article 28 promises that school discipline will be "administered in a manner consistent with the child's human dignity and in conformity with the present Convention." When pared to the core, the convention allows for no discipline whatsoever. Therefore, we can assume that behavioral problems in our schools will become much worse if this treaty becomes law. Under this treaty, any disciplinary measure must be administered "in accordance with other applicable international laws on the rights of the child." That could mean that a disruptive child could not be sent home because the treaty gives him the irrevocable right to an education. The treaty's position that all children have that right will certainly open courtroom doors for radical child-rights advocates who, for many years, have been fighting to end school suspensions and expulsions altogether. Liberal advocates presume that the rights of one delinquent child are more important than the rights of all the other children who are having their right to learn violated by one child's disruptive behavior.

Under this article, a student who has been disrespect-

ful to his teacher cannot be forced to stand in the hallway
if he considers standing in the hall an "indignity." Further, it's questionable whether "disrespect" (as defined by
the majority) is a punishable offense at all under this
treaty, given the child's "absolute and irrevocable right"
to express himself. Disobeying a teacher, name-calling, or
cursing is considered to be a minor offense by many,
given today's standards. But, such behavior is far from
insignificant and always leads to more serious problems if
students are not disciplined. When children do not fear
the consequences of bad behavior, behavior seldom im-
proves. Teachers will be faced with the difficult task of
what to do when more serious problems arise. If all articles of the treaty are enforced, there would be virtually
no way to punish students committing the very serious
offenses of cheating, stealing, fighting, or bringing weapons or drugs to school. It is beyond the realm of common
sense to believe that it is in the best interest of any child
not to administer discipline when discipline is legitimately
necessary.

Teachers with a genuine commitment to the education and welfare of children are deserving of our highest
respect. They have an incredibly difficult job to do, and
they are meagerly compensated for it. Personally, with
the exceptions of Bible teachers and parents with godly
wisdom, I can think of no task more worthy of respect
than teaching children to read, write, and reason out the
meaning of life. Those educators with strong moral and
spiritual convictions have the most difficult time of all,
and, as a parent, I am extremely grateful for their perse-
verance and commitment to all children. Without Christian teachers in the public school system, we (literally)
wouldn't have a prayer. If ratified, this legislation will
make it extremely difficult for all teachers to continue
doing their jobs.

The problem of violence in schools today keeps many
teachers who want to help children away. Every day, educators are forced against the wall as they are insulted by

students and even threatened with physical violence. Because of the cautions issued to them regarding the "rights" of children, many teachers fail to discipline bad behavior when it first begins. Thus, children grow into bullies who understand their "rights" so well, they know there will be no consequences for their actions—no matter how violent they become. You may recall the story of a thirteen-year-old New York City boy who murdered on three different occasions. After the third murder, he was finally incarcerated by authorities. When asked why he'd killed again, he shrugged his shoulders and said, "Because I got by with it the first two times."

Though that is an extreme example, it proves the point that children need discipline. And, it must be said that the very people who want to give children so many rights do not want to hold them accountable for their wrongs. This treaty will prove especially harmful to inner-city children because the incidents of violence are much higher there already. Even without the restrictions on discipline issued through the treaty, metal detectors and armed police officers testify to the violence in inner city-schools. Those children will be further victimized by even more drugs and violence, as gun and drug searches and disciplinary actions are prohibited under this law. As difficult as it is to find teachers for the inner city now, it will be even more difficult when the effects of the treaty are fully felt.

Article 29: THE RIGHT OF THE STATE TO MOLD THE PERSONALITY OF EVERY CHILD: By using outcome-based education methods, the state assumes the right to "develop your child's personality" in order to prepare him for "responsible life in a free society" and to teach him "respect for the natural environment." The thought of the likes of some politicians "developing my child's personality" makes me cringe. This same article promises to develop the child's respect for his parents, but that seems more than ludicrous and highly improbable, given the treaty's purpose.

THE RIGHT OF THE STATE TO MANDATE EDUCATION: If there is any hope of halting the Goals 2000 pace toward a national public-school curriculum, that hope will be dashed if the CRC is ratified. Repeatedly, the treaty refers to government control over the education of children and obligates signatory nations to adopt school curricula in step with the agenda of a one-world global government.

The Legal Impact of the Treaty

Under the U.S. Constitution, Article VI, Section 2 (the Supremacy Clause), "all Treaties made . . . under the Authority of the United States, shall be the supreme Law of the Land; and the Judges in every State shall be bound thereby, any Thing in the Constitution of Laws of any State to the Contrary notwithstanding."

In other words, any treaty made by a U.S. president and having a concurrence of two-thirds of the Senate is deemed "supreme law" and, as such, overrides any existing laws that conflict with it. Significantly, if this treaty is ratified, the United States will be forced to change long-standing laws pertaining to education and the family in order to cater to the demands of the United Nations. Under the convention, individual judges will be forced to decide whether they will implement a treaty that actually *surrenders* American national sovereignty to the U.N.

While the Supremacy Clause renders a treaty "supreme law of the land," treaties share that designation with the Constitution itself. Thus, the question: Are treaties subject to normal Constitutional restrictions? One would certainly assume so, given the objectives of the Constitution's framers. Alexander Hamilton declared, "The only constitutional exception to the power of making treaties is that it shall not change the Constitution . . . a treaty which should manifestly betray or sacrifice primary interest of the state would be null."[11] A Supreme Court decision in 1890 (*DeGeoffrey v. Riggs*) clearly established that treaties may not contradict the Constitution. But, in

1950, the Supreme Court ruled that a valid treaty overrides state law on matters otherwise within state control (*Missouri v. Holland*).

Douglas Phillips is an attorney and director of Government Affairs for the National Center for Home Education. Speculating on the Supreme Court's position regarding parental rights, Mr. Phillips writes, "The most likely scenario is that the courts will deem the 'rights' articulated in the treaty to be consistent with the Constitution. It seems unlikely that the same Court which has consistently upheld a woman's 'right to privacy' as defined by *Roe vs. Wade*, will strike down a children's rights measure."* While it's impossible to know for certain how the Supreme Court will rule on the parental rights questions posed by this treaty, we must consider whether or not the United States is willing to gamble with such radical legislation.

The Bricker Amendment was offered as a constitutional amendment to the Supremacy Clause. It proposed that "a treaty which conflicts with the Constitution shall not be of any force or effect. . . . A treaty shall become effective as internal law in the United States only through legislation which would be valid in the absence of the treaty." The amendment was rejected, which causes one to wonder why congressmen and congresswomen, allegedly interested in protecting the rights of American citizens, would oppose an amendment which secures the effectiveness of the U.S. Constitution?

Under Article 4, states will be legally bound to enforce the treaty. The United States would be bound to "undertake all appropriate legislative, administrative, and other measures for the implementation of the rights recognized in this Convention . . . within the framework of international co-operation." Since the United States was

---

* "United Nations Convention on the Rights of the Child," special report, National Center for Home Education.

founded, the responsibility of parents to raise and protect their children has been an established principle of constitutional law. By way of example, read the U.S. Supreme Court's 1979 decision, *Parham v. J.R.*, in which Chief Justice Warren Burger, writing for the majority, commented:

> Our jurisprudence history has reflected Western Civilization concepts of the family as a unit with broad parental authority over minor children. Our cases have consistently followed that course . . . historically it has been recognized that the natural bonds of affection lead parents to act in the best interests of their children. . . .
>
> That some parents "may at times be acting against the interests of their children" creates a basis for caution, but it is hardly a reason to discard wholesale those pages of human experience that teach that parents generally do act in the children's best interest. . . . The statist notion that government power should supersede parental authority in *all* cases because *some* parents abuse and neglect children is repugnant to American tradition.[12]

Until now, the right of competent parents to raise their own children has never been questioned, nor has the idea of complete autonomy for minor children ever been seriously debated in the national political arena. With the intrusion of the one-world government philosophy into the lives of the American people, it is clear that this treaty, if ratified, will impose international law on the "free" citizens of this country—law which stands to render the U.S. Constitution ineffectual to protect Americans from the invasion of foreign governments onto our soil and into our homes. As Douglas Phillips says in his special report on the subject, "The Convention on the Rights of the Child cannot be reconciled with the clear precedents of American law and tradition."

What Will Ratification Mean to Parents?

As stated previously, the implications of the convention are so broad that children could easily sue their parents for any reason, alleging "neglect." The CRC defines "neglect" as the parent's failure to comply with any of the child's rights or standards set forth in the treaty—an extremely general definition in anyone's terms. And, as states will be treaty-bound to investigate and, ultimately, prosecute *all* allegations, we can only imagine the long-range ramifications.

Parents who home-school will be prime targets for state investigations as social workers will level even more charges of "neglect," given the government's presupposition that home-schooled children are not "properly socialized." The CRC will give government all the ammunition it needs to go after home-schooling parents by claiming that their children are being denied their right to "freedom of association" with others. Further, home-schooling parents with moral values different from that of the government's will most certainly be deemed "negligent" under this law.

Parent Police

The thrust of the CRC is toward usurping parent's rights while subjecting them to close government scrutiny. If this treaty becomes law, we can expect further government intrusion into the private sector and more taxation as huge bureaucracies are created to investigate the complaints of children who are angry with their parents. Implicit to the convention is the requirement that signatory nations will enforce this children's rights measure by policing parents. Toward that end, Article 43 calls for the appointment of a panel of ten "experts" (the Committee on the Rights of the Child) to oversee implementation of the treaty and "generate a permanent dialogue involving all parties concerned with . . . children's rights."

The treaty claims that members of the committee will be chosen for their "high moral standing and recognized competence in the field" of children's rights, but it doesn't define what "high moral standing" or "competence" is. Could Ted Kennedy sit on this panel? What about Michael Jackson or Joycelyn Elders? How about Faye Wattleton, president of Planned Parenthood? All claim to be advocates of children.

Whoever these "parent police" are, it's safe to say that no one would be appointed to this committee who disagrees with any of the treaty's provisions, so that certainly eliminates all Christians who embrace biblical principles and the idea that God's Word is the Ultimate Authority. Whoever is chosen, those who sit on the committee will be responsible for "monitoring" each nation. And, each nation will be required to submit a regular report of its "progress" regarding the implementation of children's rights as set forth in the treaty.

Article 3 issues the standards by which government will evaluate parental conduct. It states that "in all actions concerning children, whether undertaken by public or private social welfare institutions, courts of law, administrative authorities or legislative bodies, the best interest of the child shall be a primary consideration." Nowhere in that section does the article mention "parents."

Section 2 of Article 3 declares that "States Parties" shall "undertake to ensure the child such protection and care as is necessary." The architects of the document did allow parents the courtesy of saying they will "take our rights and duties into account," but, in the end, the treaty gives the state the indisputable right to "take all appropriate legislative and administrative measures on behalf of the child in question." If a government agent determines that "appropriate legislative and administrative measures" means that your child should be taken from you and placed under the full supervision of the state, you and your child will stand defenseless against the court's ruling.

You, the Child Abuser

Scripture gives many examples of the parents' need and responsibility to discipline their children. In Old Testament times, incorrigible children were dealt with severely.[13] Repeatedly, God exhorts parents to discipline their children with love and to "train them up in the way they should go." Often, training requires discipline, and, when appropriate, discipline should be applied—including spanking. In His wisdom, God made no provision for child's rights advocacy laws in a world ruled by the Prince of Darkness. It was never God's intention for godless bureaucrats to raise His children! God reserved the job of parenting for those to whom He gave the children.

Since behaviors heretofore considered "rebellious" will be viewed simply as a child "exercising his rights," we can expect to see a radical increase in the number of "child abuse" cases leveled against parents who accept their biblical responsibility to punish disobedient children. Under this treaty, spanking could well be interpreted as child abuse. Article 2, Section 2, ensures that children are "protected against all forms of discrimination or punishment." Presumably, that would include spanking, taking away privileges, or "grounding" a child—a punishment which, it could also be argued, impinges upon his rights to freedom of association and assembly. Inasmuch as the treaty demands that discipline be "administered in a manner consistent with the child's dignity" (though the treaty does not define what that means) your child will have legal grounds to sue you if he feels a spanking is undignified, and he'd probably win! Since government assumes the role of parent under this treaty and, thus, has the right to determine what's "best" for your child, it's not absurd to think that, given the state's liberal bent, the court may consider *any* punishment child abuse.

Indoctrination

Assuming that the treaty will be ratified, the National Council for the Social Studies is currently pushing to have the contents of the U.N. Convention on the Rights of the Child taught in all social studies classes throughout America. Several articles have already been published in educational journals that instruct teachers in ways to incorporate the U.N. convention into existing curriculum. (In case a parent should assume to impose his values or punishment on a child, the council wants to make sure your child "knows his rights.") Through her Amnesty International Urgent Action letters, Ellen Moore coaches teachers in "practical ways to involve children in exercising their rights." Since the term *involvement* indicates action, we can assume that teachers will be coaching our children in the fine art of rebellion—often, without even realizing that they're doing it!

In reading the countless articles aimed at teachers, it's easy to see how anyone could be misled who had not read the treaty itself. Indeed, I feel safe in saying that those who wrote the articles did not read the treaty in most cases; it is much more likely that they read the U.N.'s literature on the treaty. In a report to educators on the subject, William Fernekes suggests that a study of the convention is "integral to realizing major citizenship goals of the social studies." If Mr. Fernekes actually read the treaty, he would know that one thing has absolutely nothing to do with the other. If he did read the treaty, we have a bigger problem because he goes on to laud the merits of "an enlightened, participatory citizenry" while ignoring the fact that the treaty does not make children participatory at all. Rather, it relegates them to state servitude and dependence on government. If that is what mainstream educators want for the future Americans, we're in worse trouble than I thought.

Fernekes recommends that teachers "introduce students early in their education to the major components of the CRC and that they systematically study those components." He claims it "is sensible to have young people . . . examine the rights afforded to them in the CRC and the extent to which our federal government advocates its ratification. It makes sense to permit young people to challenge the structures of authority . . . by using the rights in the convention as a starting point for . . . deliberation." This is not a course in social studies as much as an opportunity for liberal educators to inspire rebellion against all types of authority. It is absolutely appalling to me that many school children are studying the U.N. convention—which is not even law yet in this country—when fewer and fewer of them ever study (let alone *see*) a copy of the United States Constitution.

Currently, there is an all-out effort to convince teachers of the dire need for ratification of this treaty. It's difficult to pick up any educational journal without finding some reference to the convention and its "importance to the welfare of all children in America." (Remember, many of those journals are published by the NEA, which shares the socialist philosophy of the U.N.) It is doubtful that any significant number of teachers will request a copy of the U.N. treaty and study it thoroughly. Indeed, most people would not, and proponents know that. Unless teachers and parents are made aware of the implications of this treaty, it will most certainly become the Law of the Land.

Nigel Cantwell is an organizational consultant who helped draft the CRC. While trying to convince teachers of the document's validity, he openly admits that Article 15 (which grants the irrevocable right to freedom of association) "is arguably potentially dangerous for children and promotes an extraordinarily laissez-faire attitude."[14]

One should question the logic: What kind of people create laws to "protect children" and then turn around and admit that those laws are "potentially dangerous"?

That's equivalent to handing a small child a box of matches
and a can of gasoline and telling him to make a fire so he
can keep warm! In accord with that same logic, Article 38
of this treaty, which claims to be in the best interest of
every child, mandates every child over the age of fifteen
to pick up arms and go to war.

Ironically, many proponents of this treaty are the first
to admit that much of the destruction done to children
"is done directly by agencies either of the state or accred-
ited by the state. Much, too," they admit, "is done indi-
rectly by our political and economic system."[15] Having
said that, how could these "advocates" expect to be found
credible while favoring legislation that will dramatically
increase government's ability to interfere in the welfare
of children?

Entitlements or Rights?

A myriad of (additional) "free" state-induced programs
and services are introduced under the CRC—all designed
to encourage parents to relinquish their responsibility to
protect, educate, and raise their children and give that
right to the state. The treaty seeks to lure public support
by providing state-subsidized day-care facilities for two-
income families, giving mothers incentive to entrust their
children to state agents while they go to work outside the
home. This means that children will be raised to assume
the humanistic values of government and not the biblical
values God has commanded parents to teach.

The Constitution of the United States of America
does not issue "economic rights" to any citizen, but the
U.N. treaty does. Because the United States is a compassionate nation under God, we have made provisions, independent of the U.N., for the economically disadvan-
taged. Those provisions are called "entitlements," and
entitlements are *not rights*—they are benefits given by free
citizens until the majority agree that enough is enough.
Entitlements are implemented through law and withdrawn

the same way. No American has an inherent right to financial assistance as this treaty supposes.

Pushing for ratification are radical left-wing organizations that want to increase welfare benefits. At the forefront is Marian Wright Edelman, founder of the Children's Defense Fund, and former CDF chairman Hillary Clinton. Both are unrelenting in their criticism of the "decade of indifference" (the Reagan-Bush years), during which time they allege that government forgot the poor kids and spent all our money on weapons. Pleading her case dramatically and convincingly—unless one has all the facts—Edelman says government spent too much on defense "while letting the internal enemies of poverty, joblessness, violence, family disintegration, and hopelessness rage unabated . . . We should stop this picking on young children."

The rhetoric is touching, but Edelman was so busy choosing words that would incite politicians to open the state wallet that she forgot to look at the facts: Since 1981, spending on Aid to Families with Dependent Children has risen by 28 percent in real terms. Food stamp outlays are up 33 percent, those for Head Start and related programs by 23 percent. For child-related nutrition programs, the amount increased 97 percent with Medicaid benefits up by 199 percent—hardly indicative of an "indifferent" administration!

If the CDF's idea of increased spending is such a good one, maybe they could explain why the child-poverty rate has increased by almost 8 percent since the big spending began in 1960?[16] Could it be because government continues to financially reward women who have illegitimate children? Does Edelman, and those who share her views, know that more than 50 percent of the children living in poverty, live in single-family homes, as opposed to 10 percent who live with both parents?

Goose-stepping with the socialist architects of the U.N. treaty, the CDF wants to make government the head of the house. The organization says it's concerned with "the lack of strong families and communities," but what it does is fight for *more* welfare, which they know creates more dependence and state presence in communities where there are no men. Again, it's typical liberal double-speak: What they *say* and what they actually *do* are diametrically opposed. With their mouths, liberal, child-rights advocates say they have the best interest of children at heart, but what they do is give more financial incentives to women who have babies out of wedlock, enabling them to bear more children who will eventually grow up in poverty. Thus, the term "welfare-poverty-cycle."

The question is, how much is enough? How long does the working class have to work in order to keep paying for those the government subsidizes not to work? Following the largest tax increase in United States history under Bill Clinton, could it be that the hidden agenda of the far Left is suddenly exposed under the light of reality? When those who have always existed apart from welfare are taxed so highly that they can't afford to live without government subsidies themselves, we will be a socialist nation.

No one wants to see a child hungry or hurt. But, the way to break the poverty cycle is not to keep pouring money into programs that aren't working in order to address real problems. The way to protect children from poverty is to stop rewarding illegitimacy and to make work and/or education a prerequisite for receiving welfare benefits. State welfare programs only perpetuate feelings of dependency and hopelessness—which is exactly what socialists want. Pride results from knowledge gained through education; self-sufficiency comes from diligence and hard work. Throwing money at the poor until we become a nation of poor people is not the answer. For all her flowery rhetoric and two-hanky appeals, if Edelman really cares about children, she will quit encouraging the poor to expect something for nothing and teach them the biblical principles of self-sufficiency, diligence, and hard work. God is far more able than government; those who trust in Him will always find peace and His measure of prosperity.

Other organizations that support the U.N. convention:

• The United Nations Education, Scientific and Cultural Organization (UNESCO)—an organization so radical that the U.S. withdrew its membership in 1984.

• The Education Development Center, Inc., infamous for its globalist curricula and prohomosexual and pornographic sex-education programs.

• The highly funded educational establishment, directed by the National Education Association.

• UNICEF calls itself the "child advocate for the world's children," and few will argue that the organization has done much to feed starving children around the world. But the recent tag-line used in UNICEF's public service announcements reveals much more about its real purpose when the announcer proclaims, "Every child is *our* child" (emphasis added). UNICEF is, after all, the United Nations International Children's Emergency Fund.

Conclusion

This treaty seems so radical, it's almost impossible to believe that it will ever be ratified, but it is actually dangerously close. After President Clinton signs the treaty (he has said that he will), it will bypass the House and go directly to the Senate where, at this writing, it is less than twenty votes away from becoming law! The American people must act immediately to stop the United Nations Convention on the Rights of the Child, or the traditional Christian family will move even further toward extinction.

There is no disputing that our children face problems today that most of us could never have imagined, apart from the hints given in George Orwell's *1984*. But, what they *don't* need is more freedom. On the contrary, children need boundaries and the security that loving discipline brings. No one has stated the need for limits more eloquently than Dr. W.N. Kirby, commissioner of education in Austin, Texas. In a speech given in 1987, he said, "Young people search for the limits. They are confused and distorted when limits are not set. We must teach our young people that the limits are where they have always been. The great moral truths of mankind never change. Man can ignore them . . . but they are always there."

God knows better than any humanistic state what is necessary for raising healthy, productive members of society. This treaty purports to do to the United States exactly what Lenin did in his effort to establish a communist Russia.

What You Can Do

Inform your pastor of the U.N. Convention on the Rights of the Child and the implications the treaty will have on the family; ask him to inform your congregation. Perhaps he will allow a brief synopsis of the treaty's contents to be included as an insert in your weekly bulletin. Or, invite a guest speaker informed on this subject to address your congregation or a group of parents in your church. It can also be effective to call local secular and Christian radio and television stations and ask why they haven't covered this important issue. If they have covered it, implore them to do more in an effort to keep the issue before the public until the treaty is voted on.

Local and national ministries focused on issues that affect the family should also be called and written. Ask them to become involved in fighting ratification of the U.N. Convention.

Give information about the treaty to everyone you know—Christians and non-Christians; if passed, this treaty will have a devastating effect on all families.

Organize your community to call and write your senators and any representatives *in* or *of* government who may be able to influence a senator's vote on the treaty. If you write or speak to a senator directly, tell him or her that you stand in radical opposition to Senate Resolution 70, and ask how the senator plans to vote once Clinton signs the treaty. If they favor the treaty, ask them to explain their position, and question whether they've read the document in its entirety. If you disagree with the implications of this treaty, flood the White House with letters stating your opposition. There is no time to waste! If you disagree with the ratification of the U.N. Convention on the Rights of the Child, you must act now!

Endnotes

1. Proverbs 19:18

2. James P. Lucier, Ph.D., "Unconventional Rights Children and the United Nations," *Family Policy*, a publication of the Family Research Council, Washington, D.C. (August 1992), 5.

3. World Declaration on the Survival, Protection and Development of Children and Plan of Action for implementing the World Declaration on the Survival, Protection and Development of Children in the 1990s, United Nations, New York (30 September 1990), 1.

4. Ibid., 4.

5. Kenneth Jost, "Children's Legal Rights," *CQ Researcher* (23 April 1993): 432.

6. Beatrice and Ronald Gross, *The Children's Rights Movement: Overcoming the Oppression of Young People* (Garden City, N.Y.: Anchor Press, Doubleday), 207.

7. Lucier, "Unconventional Rights," 7.

8. Ibid.

9. Douglas Phillips, "United Nations Convention on the Rights of the Child," special report, National Center for Home Education, 8.

10. Nigel Cantwell, "Conventionally Theirs: An Overview of the Origins, Content, and Significance of the Convention of the Rights of the Child," *Social Education* (April/May 1992): 207.

11. Richard B. Morse, *Alexander Hamilton and the Founding of the Nation,* as quoted by Douglas Phillips, JD., in his report, "The Legal Impact of the United Nations Convention on the Rights of the Child," 1.

12. Quoted by Douglas Phillips, "United Nations Convention," 12-13.

13. Exodus 21:15.

14. Cantwell, "Conventionally Theirs," 207.

15. Beatrice and Gross, *Children's Rights,* 13.

16. Daniel Seligman, "Measuring PC," *Fortune Magazine* (19 April 1993): 159.

8

Where Do We Go from Here?

There will be terrible times in the last days.
—2 Timothy 3:1

Few would deny that these are terrible times. Numerous climactic and political events around the world are keeping scholars speculating about the imminent fulfillment of biblical prophecy and the ultimate return of Christ. Many will argue that the current trend toward globalism is a clear indication of the beginning of the end times. Indeed, many of the elements necessary for the implementation of a one-world government are already in place. As Timothy prophesied, the world is now full of false prophets and godless men and women who oppose the truth.

Our children are being educated in a public school system where they are "always learning, but never acknowledging the truth."[1] One cannot watch an evening newscast or read a daily paper without being reminded that people have become "abusive, ungrateful, unholy, without self-control, brutal, not lovers of the good, treacherous, and lovers of pleasure rather than lovers of God."

Man is now exactly as Timothy prophesied he would
become in the last days.[2]

At the very least, it is clear that the United States is in
the midst of a moral and ethical dilemma.

But, those attempting to interpret the signs of the
times and to calculate the number of days remaining
must also ask themselves what God expects them to do as
they wait.

> Continue in him, so that when he appears we may
> be confident and unashamed before him at his
> coming. (1 John 2:28)

Those who believe in a sovereign God must recognize
His power to deliver this nation from the hands of the
enemy. Those who understand God's justice can rest in
the confidence that those who oppose Him now will face
eternal consequences far worse than any punishment man
can impose. The assurance that vengeance belongs to the
Lord can be a blessing and a curse—a blessing because we
can know that justice will prevail, but a curse because that
knowledge sometimes leads to spiritual smugness. For
too long, Christians have sat quietly in churches all across
America as the enemies of God have boldly entered the
arenas of politics and education.

We can no longer seek sanctuary behind the four
walls of our homes and churches. Now, the cultural war
is raging, and the enemy is quickly advancing; Christians
are being called to leave their comfort zones and take a
firm stand in the camp of the enemy. We want a return
to traditional morality and an end to moral relativism.
We want our schools back. We want our streets back.
Our government belongs to "We, the people . . ." and we
want it back! And, we want our nation and political policy
restored to the biblical principles upon which the United
States was founded. We claim God's promise for the
United States of America:

> I will make you into a great nation and I will bless
> you; I will make your name great, and you will be

a blessing. I will bless those who bless you, and
whoever curses you I will curse; and all peoples on
earth will be blessed through you. (Gen. 12:2)

Knowing that God will ultimately win does not release believers from their responsibility to defend (and
contend for) God's morality in the world in which we
live. America has been greatly blessed because America
has always been a blessing to other nations. Now, our
own citizens are spiritually dead and wounded as a result
of the tragic effects of the cultural war, and we must be
a blessing to them. We have a responsibility to defend the
innocent, who are being ravaged by the armies of humanism and immorality. There *are moral absolutes*, and those
absolutes must be defended.

Children have an absolute right to grow up unbur-
dened by thoughts of sexual perversion and unhindered
by the pressure to become sexually active before marriage. They have an absolute right to be informed of, and
to believe in, God's plan for the family as He designed
the family to be. And, children fortunate enough to live
in the United States of America have an absolute right to
an education that will equip them to read and understand the Holy Scriptures. And, God has ordained that
children have an absolute right to be raised by their own
parents. When the state attempts to usurp that right, the
state invites rebellion.

Slowly, American citizens are losing their constitutional freedoms of religion, free speech, and the right to
bear arms to protect themselves. Godless politicians are
working overtime to destroy a nation built upon biblical
principles. Policy-makers who are enemies of the traditional American family have set their wills against the will
of God, and the destruction they have wrought can only
be rectified when they are voted out of office and replaced by men with godly wisdom. At this writing, the
Constitution, *as written by our Founding Fathers*, is still law,
and its intent is still clear: God ordained the United States

of America to be a free country—not a socialist state.
Those willing to defend their rights will, by the power of
God, reclaim what is rightfully theirs.

The collapse of soviet communism and the impend-
ing collapse of socialism throughout Europe should send
a clear message to the radical Left in this country, that
the human spirit cannot be made subject to any man.
There has never been a government throughout history
that has stood opposed to God and survived. America
survives, in spite of itself, because of the fact that this
nation grew out of biblical precepts. It still exists because
of the millions of Christians who continue to do God's
will and to pray for the restoration of this great country.

> If you return to the Almighty, you will be restored:
> If you remove wickedness far from your tent . . .
> (Job 22:23)

> If you repent, I will restore you that you may serve
> me; if you utter worthy, not worthless, words, you
> will be my spokesman. Let this people turn to you,
> but you must not turn to them. (Jer. 15:19)

No social problem exists that God's people, through
His power, cannot rectify; when God is with us, no one
can stand against us! The real challenge we face is not in
restoring a society because only God can do that. The
believer's challenge lies in keeping our *focus* straight. As
concerned parents and citizens of a nation under siege,
we know we will never completely "right" the world, nor
will we ever rid the world of sin, but neither should be
our goal. Our goal is to focus on Jesus, tell the truth, and
then trust God to move in the hearts of those He chooses
to take action within their own communities. The primary reason for involvement in any political or social
cause should be to show others the person of Jesus Christ,
to demonstrate His truth and love, and to explain His
purpose.

Cornelius Van Til, the great Christian apologist and
professor at Westminster Theological Seminary, taught

that, when pared down, all authority is religious. Similarly, all public policy is religious. Therefore, we will either be governed by a humanist religion, which professes man-as-God, or true Christianity, which believes that God is God.[3] It is ridiculous to think that morality cannot be legislated. Clearly, morality is being legislated every day. The question is, Whose morality is it? If those of us who believe in traditional morality and the preservation of biblical precepts do not pay closer attention to politics and take immediate action to reverse the moral tide in America, our fate will be sealed by our own hands.

There is no question that those who fight the cultural war will suffer for what they believe. As biblical prophesy is being fulfilled, Christians who take a stand for God will be persecuted on every front. They will be mocked, humiliated, verbally and sometimes physically attacked. Every war has an emotional toll to pay, and spiritual wars are no different. But, lest the reader throw up hands in surrender, the Lord encourages you:

> Do not be terrified; do not be afraid. . . . The Lord your God, who is going before you, will fight for you. (Deut. 1:29-30)

Believers need not fear those who can destroy the body because the weapons we fight with are not the weapons of the world. On the contrary, they have divine power to demolish strongholds![4] Indeed, "We are hard pressed on every side, but not crushed; perplexed, but not in despair; persecuted, but not abandoned; struck down, but not destroyed."[5] As believers in the Word of God (and with all the power *that* implies) and as citizens of a country founded upon biblical principles, we make a choice whether or not to tolerate the destruction of traditional morality and the progressive annihilation of Christianity. Clearly, the voices of millions of Christian and conservative parents in America cannot be ignored—especially when they express their disapproval as one body! Individual believers will either choose to surrender to the

forces of evil or they will put on the full armour of God
and stand up boldly to face the enemy! These are not
times without hope for those who believe in the God of
the Bible—and in His power to act on behalf of His people.
Where there is God, there is great hope.

There is a way to battle the forces of humanism and
despair. There is hope for a nation that has shaken its fist
in the face of God: The way is through prayer, and the
hope is through action. The destruction of the American
family is only imminent if Christians refuse to claim the
power that is theirs through the Holy Spirit. There is
nothing to fear for those who enter the battle dressed in
the full armor of God and well informed of the tactics of
the enemy. That is not to say that we won't lose some
battles; we will. That is not to say that we will not be
wounded; we will. Many of us will suffer, and some of our
soldiers will fall on the battleground, but not one of us
will perish.

Certainly, if we view life only in the context of the
issues addressed here, our future as a nation looks bleak.
Therefore, it's imperative to remember that our joy is not
dependent upon our circumstances, but lies in our saving
faith in Jesus Christ and our anticipation of eternal life
with Him; our hope is not in this world, but in the next.
However, our confidence in eternal life does not negate
our responsibility to be watchmen on the wall and con-
tenders for the faith.

All readers fortunate enough to live in towns across
America that still embrace the values of traditional academics and morality are encouraged to thank the Lord
every day; you are becoming a privileged minority. To
the wonderful and devoted educators still committed to
teaching literacy and the Judeo-Christian values: We thank
God for you; you are a blessing to our communities and
to our children. As the enemy continues to advance, it
will become more and more difficult for communities to
maintain their constitutional rights and to prevent state
intrusion in the personal lives of their residents. And, it

will become even more difficult for individual educators to stand their ground and face the growing opposition head-on. Therefore, it becomes an even greater imperative to remember that when God is with us, no one can stand against us.

The Power of Prayer

> I looked for a man among them who would build up the wall and stand before me in the gap on behalf of the land so I would not have to destroy it, but I found none. So I will pour out my wrath on them and consume them with my fiery anger, bringing down on their own heads all they have done, declares the sovereign Lord. (Ezek. 22:30, 31)

God was willing to save an entire nation in exchange for one man who was willing to intercede with Him on behalf of the people. The most valuable weapon in the cultural war is prayer.

> What other nation is so great as to have their gods near them the way the Lord our God is near us whenever we pray to him? And what other nation is so great as to have such righteous decrees and laws as this body of laws I am setting before you today. Only be careful, and watch yourselves closely so that you do not forget the things your eyes have seen or let them slip from your heart as long as you live. Teach them to your children and to their children after them. (Deut. 4:7-9)

If you are a prayer warrior in this cultural war, God's army is deeply indebted to you. Without the prayers of the righteous, this nation could truly not survive.

The First Amendment grants all Americans the freedom to express ourselves, and that freedom cannot be restricted by government—even as it pertains to prayer. The Constitution guarantees Christians the right to pray and to share the gospel in public places. All children have a legal right to pray in school. Though school-sponsored religious activities are forbidden, no one has the right to prevent your child from praying by himself or with others. Government dictating that man cannot pray is equivalent to government telling a man he may not think.

The phrase "separation of church and state" is worn out and irrelevant when it comes to the matter of public prayer. "Congress shall make no law respecting an establishment of religion, or prohibiting the free exercise thereof." Further, the phrase "separation of church and state" is not found in the Constitution of the United States, nor is it even found in the notes of the Constitutional Convention; it was first used by Thomas Jefferson in an address to the Danbury Baptist Association thirteen years *after* the Constitution was written.[6]

Dressed for Battle

The lies of the liberal Left are being exposed throughout every realm of society, as failure in every quarter proves that bigger, more intrusive government does not work. The American spirit will never succumb to the stranglehold of socialism. Legislation that attempts to restrict individual freedom and rights to privacy must be met with the public disdain it deserves. Government programs and agencies which contribute to the moral decay of America must be replaced with those that reflect the values of the majority. The deadly AIDS virus has left hundreds of thousands of corpses as gruesome testimony to the fact that, when a society lowers its standards to accommodate perversity, it is in danger of losing its life. The absence of moral education has led to a society wrought with violent crime—a result of the elimination of God and biblical mandate from the public realm. One abiding Truth—that the God of the Bible *does* exist, and that His precepts are good and righteous; and life for every man—is the hope for an entire nation.

Knowing Your Rights

Because the establishment of a national curriculum violates constitutional law, it is presumed that a school district that is denied federal funds for not using OBE curricula would challenge the government in court. I have found nothing in my research to indicate that such a challenge has yet been leveled, but the law is new. According to the Rutherford Institute, there are, at this writing, several cases pending where parents are challenging use of personal questionnaires and psychological tests administered without prior written parental consent (in violation of the Grassley Amendment). A couple of cases failed to make it to court because the school districts involved agreed to drop the tests.

Parents must approach local superintendents and curriculum directors about their curricula concerns. They must request copies of all tests and questionnaires and study them carefully. When authorities are responsive, as they often are, change is easy and effective and relatively quick. When authorities are uncooperative, confrontation becomes necessary, and parents must stand firm. As Dr. Bob Simonds, president of Citizens for Excellence in Education, points out, "Position and control go to the administration. Votes go to the parents. For every teacher, there are about sixty parents. Guess who ultimately wins!"

Know the names of your school board members, and know what they think about the curriculum the district is using. If the courses are objectionable, let the board know how you feel. If the material is not changed to reflect the values of your community, voters must organize and make *their* objections heard when board members run for re-election. On the federal level, know the names of your congressmen and congresswomen and make sure they know yours! Write letters, call the Capitol Hill switchboard, and make your voice heard on every issue that concerns you.

If conservative parents are not involved, it's usually because they're uninformed. The job of the activist is to get them informed and make sure they have the right facts. Parents want and deserve a voice in public education; these are our children, lent by God, who is the Ultimate Parent—they do not belong to the state!

Just as government cannot force children to attend schools where Christianity is taught, they do not have a right to force-feed children the religion of humanism or doctrines of homosexuality or sexual promiscuity. Schools are teaching those doctrines because parents are sitting quietly by and letting them do it. Parents must *demand* a return to traditional academic curricula and the teaching of moral absolutes. We can't afford to keep letting our children walk innocently into the dens of lions.

It's imperative to remember that government is made up of people—"WE, the people . . ." If we don't like the way the government is doing things, we can let politicians know that on election day.

Indeed, if Goals 2000 and the U.N. Convention on the Rights of the Child are part of God's plan to usher in the last days, nothing will stop God's plan. If both are vessels to move America toward the one-world government described in the Bible, the best we can hope for is godly wisdom and spiritual discernment as we wait for Christ's return. Though we may, indeed, be approaching the end-times, Scripture says that a thousand years to man is like a blinking of the eye to God. That said, we must be alert and responsible and "occupy until he comes."

Final Determinations

Today, sex education is taught in 75 percent of our public schools, and, ironically, the number of school-based clinics has grown so rapidly, they seem to be reproducing on their own. Since SIECUS and Planned Parenthood began their heinous assault on public school children with their "morals neutral" idea of sex-ed, the illegitimacy rate has increased by 51 percent,[7] and there has been a threefold increase in the number of sexually transmitted diseases reported each year.[8]

Parents must question who gave SIECUS the right to mandate that little children be educated in immorality? Imagine for a moment a neighbor telling your child how to masturbate or explaining how homosexuals have sex. You'd be outraged! Yet, SIECUS, under the protective umbrella of the United States government, is telling your children those things and more. Now, SIECUS must be dismantled, and the responsibility for teaching morality reserved for parents, who have a right to teach their own values to their own children! If sex-ed is offered at all, it must be offered within the context of moral precepts and restricted to abstinence-only curricula because it is proven that abstinence is the only thing that works.

If the majority of parents decide that homosexual curricula are necessary at all, programs should be developed which encourage counseling approaches that address that problem without condoning the lifestyle. Programs must affirm morality. Courses should not deny the fact that less than 2 percent of people are attracted to members of the same sex, but recognition of that fact should never be confused with acceptance of the homosexual lifestyle. Students who claim to be homosexual should be counseled regarding self-restraint and should be told the truth about the psychological and medical consequences of acting on their impulses. Like adultery or sex with multiple partners, homosexuals can choose not to engage in sexual sin—not to act on their desires. The stress and confusion these children feel should never be underestimated or made light of—nor should the compassionate counselor's ability to influence the child toward change.

Parents must do everything within their power to see that schools are staffed with counselors and teachers who affirm heterosexual relationships and traditional moral values.

Regarding homosexual literature in public school libraries, if parents fail in their efforts to have such books removed, they must insist that public schools that have prohomosexual books like *Daddy's Roommate* and *Heather Has Two Mommies* also have an equal number of Bible stories for children of the same age group. Liberals who "don't want Christian values forced on their children" must stop to consider the tragic effects that have resulted from their forcing their values on children! Those who want to teach their children about homosexuality have that right—but they do *not* have the right to force that knowledge on other people's children!

Parents must assault the morals-neutral curricula being forced upon our children and insist that if it is "unconstitutional" to teach traditional Judeo-Christian values (once the staple in public schools), it is also a violation of church and state to continue teaching the religion of secular humanism. While those who oppose the current trend in public education have the option of placing their children in private schools, not everyone can afford to do that. Further, as equal contributors to the $493 billion education tab each year,[9] why should we have to? Public education began in America because godly statesmen recognized the need for every child to learn to read the Scriptures. Why should those who still embrace the philosophy of our Founding Fathers be forced out of the public schools they founded in that interest? And, though removing your child from public school is one solution to the problem of Goals 2000, it is only a temporary one; no one knows how long it will be before government invades home and private schools as well.

Biblical teaching is the parent's highest imperative. Unless your child is spiritually strong, the temporary solution offered by a private school will not prepare him for life in a society of individuals grown and "nurtured" in a values-neutral environment. Everyone will be affected by Goals 2000 because all must coexist with those indoctrinated in the humanist dogma and socialist mindset—if, in fact, Goals 2000 survives the cultural war! The architects of Goals 2000 admit that without the cooperation of the masses, their "goals will remain nothing more than a distant unattainable vision." Likewise, those of us who survived the public school system with our cognitive skills intact know that Goals 2000 will fail without public support.

How to Examine Curricula

All parents have a legal right to examine the school district's curricula. Too often, parents who request information or make inquiries are made to feel intimidated by teachers and administrators. Parents pay the salaries of public school employees, and they pay for the materials that allow them to do their jobs. Parents have every right to question, and they should. In doing so, they must remember that they can only be intimidated if they allow themselves to be.

Curriculum is most effectively evaluated using a committee of concerned parents and grandparents. Senior citizens are always excellent additions to these committees; many of them are grandparents and, thus, still have a vested interest in public education. It takes a great deal of time to study curriculum thoroughly, and senior citizens usually have more of that than young moms and dads do. In addition, they bring years of life experience which can be a real blessing to young parents who often get frustrated and impatient with the system.

The state of Arkansas requires that evolution be taught as fact when science proves that it is only theory. Parents have every right to challenge that—and any other false doctrine their children are being fed. School districts must be held accountable for what they're teaching. If teachers are not telling the truth—whether it be about evolution or AIDS—they must be held accountable! Districts that allow prohomosexual projects or guest speakers who are offensive to the majority must be made to explain themselves to parents and students. Superintendents and administrators should be forewarned that if they continue to ignore the desires of the majority, the majority is prepared to present vigorous opposition—in a court of law if necessary.

Check to see what (if any) sex-ed curriculum your school district is using. Secure the textbook and read it thoroughly; pay close attention to focus, presentation, and content. If the course includes videos or appearances by guest speakers, make an effort to view the videos beforehand—or sit in on the class when the video is shown. Learn something about the guest speakers. (Representatives from Planned Parenthood should send up red flags to parents, as should homosexuals.) Know that all sex-ed material endorsed by SIECUS promotes abortion, premarital sex, masturbation by kindergartners, tolerance of different sexual perversions, and views homosexuality as normal.

Talk to your children; ask them what they're learning, and let them know that they needn't be embarrassed telling you. If you're upset by what your child is learning, talk to the teacher personally. Ask his or her views on the sex-ed curriculum used, and ask how the material is being presented. If you disagree with the content or presentation of the material, you have a right to remove your child from the class. Work with other public school parents to improve sex-ed in your school and make your desires for abstinence-only programs known to teachers and elected officials.

If your district uses OBE curricula, ask to see a set of outcomes, and examine them closely; inquire about the district's strategy for reaching the goals. Evaluate each goal and the value of its projected outcome. For example, where "acceptance of diversity" is the goal, ask exactly what that means. Is your child expected to accept homosexuality? Premarital sex? Globalism? Your committee must also determine the academic value of the outcomes: Are children falling behind academically because too much time is being spent promoting alternative lifestyles or issues dealing with cultural pluralism? If academics appear to be suffering, inform the principal immediately, and be sure to follow up! Parents who don't see improvement quickly will want to supplement the student's learning with a private tutor or home-schooling.

Regarding assessment tests, parents have a right to see and/or protest the administration of any test that violates a child's right to privacy. Tests or student questionnaires that ask personal questions have no place in the classroom. Every child has a right to refuse to take an assessment test or to be as nebulous as he chooses when answering the questions. Parents must insist on seeing the tests your child is given. Examine the test carefully: Can it measure academic progress accurately, or is it a subjective psychological test designed to extract personal information? If you find the tests more psychologically than academically oriented, you have a right to question the motive behind the test. If your child took such a test without your written permission, the Grassley Amendment gives you grounds to implement legal action.

Parents throughout America are organizing in their efforts to take back our schools and re-educate our children in the literacy skills and moral values they're now being denied. Programs are being initiated that show great promise in the promotion of sexual abstinence curricula. In February 1994, *The Arizona Republic* reported that an increasing number of churches, celebrities, and school groups are encouraging abstinence and that, "apparently, kids are listening." To our credit, a study conducted by the University of Florida reported that "politically active, conservative Christians" are increasing their efforts to pull certain texts from classrooms or libraries.[10]

Through prayer and public action, we can eliminate school-based health clinics and Planned Parenthood's presence on public school campuses. We can eliminate the use of pornographic textbooks and sex-ed curricula that encourages study in perversity and promotes promiscuity. We can halt the expansion of Goals 2000, and we can stop ratification of the U.N. treaty if that is God's will for this nation. By exercising our constitutional right to vote, we can rid our government of the humanist, socialistically bent politicians who vote to fund the programs we oppose.

Those who stand in opposition to the status quo must be willing to accept the challenge to do things that will be ridiculed by men, but will be richly blessed when the Kingdom of God is revealed. No one can know the exact time of Christ's return. Indeed, if God has ordained that we are living in the last days, nothing we can do will change His will. But, what if this present state of affairs is a test of our faithfulness? Will we be found faithful? What will you be doing when the Lord our God returns?

> *He will keep you strong to the end, so that you will be blameless on the day of our Lord Jesus Christ. God, who has called you into fellowship with his Son Jesus Christ, our Lord, is faithful.*
>
> —1 Corinthians 1:8-9

Hallelujah! For our Lord God Almighty reigns!

Endnotes

1. 2 Timothy 3:7

2. 2 Timothy 3:2-4

3. Gary North, *Political Polytheism* (Tyler, Texas: Dominion Press, 1989).

4. 2 Corinthians 10:4-5.

5. 2 Corinthians 4:8-9

6. Jay Alan Sekulow, *Knowing Your Rights* (Washington, D.C.: Liberty, Life, and Family Publications, 1993), 18.

7. George Grant and Mark A. Horne, *Legislating Immorality* (Chicago: Moody Press, 1993), 78.

8. Dinah Richard, Ph.D., *Has Sex Education Failed Our Teenagers? A Research Report* (Pomona, CA: Focus on the Family Publishing, 1990), 24.

9. U.S. Department of Education Statistic, 1994.

10. Lee Grady, "The New X-Rated Textbooks," *Charisma* (March 1991): 60.

Order These Huntington House Books !

_____	America: Awaiting the Verdict—Mike Fuselier	4.99	_____
_____	America Betrayed—Marlin Maddoux	6.99	_____
_____	Beyond Political Correctness—David Thibodaux	9.99	_____
_____	A Call to Manhood—David E. Long	9.99	_____
_____	Conservative, American & Jewish—Jacob Neusner	9.99	_____
_____	The Dark Side of Freemasonry—Ed Decker	9.99	_____
_____	Deadly Deception: Freemasonry—Tom McKenney	8.99	_____
_____	Don't Touch That Dial—Barbara Hattemer & Robert Showers	9.99/19.99	_____
_____	En Route to Global Occupation—Gary Kah	9.99	_____
_____	*Exposing the AIDS Scandal—Dr. Paul Cameron	7.99/2.99	_____
_____	The Extermination of Christianity—Paul Schenck	9.99	_____
_____	Freud's War with God—Jack Wright, Jr.	7.99	_____
_____	Goddess Earth—Samantha Smith	9.99	_____
_____	Gays & Guns—John Eidsmoe	7.99/14.99	_____
_____	Heresy Hunters—Jim Spencer	8.99	_____
_____	Hidden Dangers of the Rainbow—Constance Cumbey	9.99	_____
_____	Hitler and the New Age—Bob Rosio	9.99	_____
_____	Homeless in America—Jeremy Reynalds	9.99	_____
_____	How to Homeschool (Yes, You!)—Julia Toto	4.99	_____
_____	Hungry for God—Larry E. Myers	9.99	_____
_____	*Inside the New Age Nightmare—Randall Baer	9.99/2.99	_____
_____	A Jewish Conservative Looks at Pagan America—Don Feder	9.99/19.99	_____
_____	A Journey into Darkness—Stephen Arrington	9.99	_____
_____	Kinsey, Sex and Fraud—Dr. Judith A. Reisman & Edward Eichel (Hard cover)	11.99	_____
_____	The Liberal Contradiction—Dale A. Berryhill	9.99	_____
_____	Legalized Gambling—John Eidsmoe	7.99	_____
_____	Loyal Opposition—John Eidsmoe	8.99	_____
_____	The Media Hates Conservatives—Dale A. Berryhill	9.99	_____
_____	Out of Control—Brenda Scott	9.99	_____
_____	Please Tell Me—Tom McKenney	9.99	_____
_____	Political Correctness—David Thibodaux	9.99	_____
_____	*The Question of Freemasonry—Ed Decker	2.99	_____
_____	Resurrecting the Third Reich—Richard Terrell	9.99	_____
_____	"Soft Porn" Plays Hardball—Dr. Judith A. Reisman	8.99/16.99	_____
_____	Subtle Serpent—Darylann Whitemarsh & Bill Reisman	9.99	_____
_____	*To Moroni With Love—Ed Decker	2.99	_____
_____	Trojan Horse—Brenda Scott & Samantha Smith	9.99	_____
_____	When the Wicked Seize a City—Chuck & Donna McIlhenny with Frank York	9.99	_____

*Available in Salt Series

Shipping & Handling _____

TOTAL _____

AVAILABLE AT BOOKSTORES EVERYWHERE or order direct from:
Huntington House Publishers•P.O. Box 53788•Lafayette, LA 70505
Send check/money order. For faster service use VISA/MASTERCARD
Call toll-free 1-800-749-4009.
Add: Freight and handling, $3.50 for the first book ordered, and $.50 for
each additional book up to 5 books.

Enclosed is $_____including postage.
VISA/MASTERCARD #_____ Exp. Date _____
Name_____ Phone: ( ) _____
Address_____
City, State, Zip_____